250

12/11

Writing Romances

A HANDBOOK BY THE
ROMANCE WRITERS OF AMERICA

Writing Romances

A HANDBOOK BY THE ROMANCE WRITERS OF AMERICA

EDITED BY RITA GALLAGHER
AND RITA CLAY ESTRADA

WRITER'S DIGEST BOOKS
CINCINNATI, OHIO

Writing Romances. Copyright © 1997 by the Romance Writers of America. Printed and bound in the United States of America. All rights reserved. No part of this book may be reproduced in any form or by any electronic or mechanical means including information storage and retrieval systems without permission in writing from the publisher, except by a reviewer, who may quote brief passages in a review. Published by Writer's Digest Books, an imprint of F&W Publications, Inc., 1507 Dana Avenue, Cincinnati, Ohio 45207. (800) 289-0963. First edition.

This hardcover edition of Writing Romances features a "self-jacket" that eliminates the need for a separate dust jacket. It provides sturdy protection for your book while it saves paper, trees and energy.

Other fine Writer's Digest Books are available from your local bookstore or direct from the publisher.

01 00 99 98 97   5 4 3 2 1

Library of Congress Cataloging-in-Publication Data

    Writing romances / the Romance Writers of America; [edited by Rita Gallagher and Rita Clay Estrada].
       p.   cm.
   Includes index.
   ISBN 0-89879-756-x (alk. paper)
   1. Love stories—Authorship. I. Gallagher, Rita. II. Estrada, Rita Clay. III. Romance Writers of America (Organization)
PN3377.5.L68W75   1996
808.3'85—dc20   96-31927
                                                                  CIP

Edited by Rita Gallagher and Rita Clay Estrada
Cover designed by Brian Roeth
Interior designed by Julie Martin

ACKNOWLEDGMENTS

With gratitude and appreciation . . .

To those stars of the romance writing firmament who took precious time away from deadlines and other commitments to share their expertise. Winners all, their knowledge and talent earned RWA Golden Heart Awards; RITA Awards, (the "Oscar" for romance writers) and the ultimate recognition—a place in the Romance Writer's Hall Of Fame. These are the keynote speakers and teachers at RWA conferences. Their shining lights are beacons, inspiring hopeful romance novelists to reach for the heavens.

There were others we wanted to ask, but bound by subject and word restrictions, we were unable to do so. Some authors, due to pressing commitments, graciously and regretfully refused.

To those who accepted, we give thanks for your time and effort expended in this project and for the love we all (published and unpublished writers alike) share for the romance genre.

To those who were forced to decline, thanks for your courtesy and good wishes.

The Editors
Rita Clay Estrada
Rita Gallagher

TABLE OF CONTENTS

ABOUT THE EDITORS

Rita Clay Estrada

Rita Clay Estrada is creator, cofounder and first president of Romance Writers of America, the largest genre writing organization in the world. In early 1980, she sold her first book to Simon and Schuster editor Kate Duffy. Since then she has published over thirty books with Silhouette, Dell, Leisure and Harlequin.

For more than four years, Rita acted as RWA spokeswoman on such programs as *CBS National News* with Steve Croft, the *Today Show*, *King TV* and *PBS National* as well as many local television and radio shows. She has given workshops and been keynote speaker at national conferences, universities and library systems throughout the country. Silhouette sent her across the Southwest and West teaching beginning writers. Harlequin flew her to Venice, Italy, to meet her fans.

She was listed in *Who's Who of American Women* in 1982, 1983 and 1984. In 1995, she was listed in *Two Thousand Notable American Women*.

Her books have won numerous awards and consistently make the national best-seller lists. The Romance Writers of America's annual published author awards were named the RITA in her honor.

Rita Gallagher

Mainstream novelist and lecturer Rita Gallagher is also a widely known novel structure teacher. Since she began teaching in 1982, over a thousand books have been sold by her former students, and more are hitting the book stands each month.

She and her daughter, Rita Clay Estrada, author of thirty-two romance novels, cofounded the world's largest writers organization, Romance Writers of America.

Gallagher was editor of the first *Romance Writer's Report*, a bimonthly magazine for members. She coordinated the first RWA conference held in 1981 at the Woodlands near Houston, Texas.

In 1984, Gallagher opened Inspiration House, a haven for aspiring writers and published novelists on deadline. Authors, poets, editors and agents joined in workshops and conferences for her

Novel Writing to Sell students. Under her tutelage, many successful authors realized their dream of becoming published writers.

Because of her remarkable track record in turning out published authors, she has been interviewed on local and national radio and television. Featured in magazines and newspapers throughout the United States, she has given seminars and workshops at colleges and writers conferences across the country.

FOREWORD

"Romance has been elegantly defined as the offspring of fiction and love -" DISRAELI

To the romance writers, and comparatively decorous dramatists of his own time, NICOLE gave the title of "public poisoners."

What is it about romance novels—and romance itself—that has always so enraged, or engaged, intellectuals and peasants alike?

Those who know, or have known, love affirm it.

"Love makes the world go 'round" is an old expression, and there are as many stories of love and romance as there are people who live them. Love is the common denominator shared by all races and creeds. It is a basic emotion inherent in the human heart. It is the balm that soothes the wounded soul, and its comforting embrace shuts out the chaos of a dissenting and often frightening society.

Romance defines the *feeling* of love. It is the wooing, the first burst of realization that, having found our other halves, our lives are changed forever. Beyond the earliest flush of recognition, romance becomes suffused with wonder that, despite our faults, someone we love loves us. As natural as the ebb and flow of tides, true love strengthens with each changing season.

Love stories and love songs have prevailed throughout the ages. Wandering minstrels throughout history sang of love, and today's pop tunes and the blues songs of country music give melodious testimony that love lives and will always live in the human heart.

It is said that cave men wooed their mates by clubbing them over the head and carrying them off to their lairs. Though clubbing in our civilized era has not the remotest connection to romance, the question arises: What motivated a cave man to choose that certain cave girl? Something in his heart, his genes, his hormones propelled him into making her "his woman." Romance!

The Trojan War was fought for Helen of Troy.

Cleopatra, Mark Anthony and Caesar knew all about romance.

Othello killed for love.

Romeo and Juliet died for it.

And, in the twentieth century, a British king gave up his throne for the love of an American woman.

Romance has always lived in the human heart and always will. It is the dream spirit born with the body. Without romance, the world can be a cold and ruthless place, fostering cynicism and bitterness. The unfathomable essence of humanity is sustained by romance. It is intertwined with our very being and cannot be dispelled—nor can it be found in the spiraling mystery of DNA.

So write your love stories! Tell the world what we as novelists all know: that romance exists and will always exist as long as humans see the sun and feel the warmth of it, as long as they smell the flowers of spring, taste the fruits of the earth, and touch the hand of a loved one.

Rita Gallagher

THE HISTORY OF ROMANCE WRITERS OF AMERICA

Rita Gallagher

Romance Writers of America (RWA) began as a dream in the minds and hearts of five published authors in a hotel room at the University of Houston's 1978 Southwest Writers' Conference.

RWA's conception was sparked by the passionate response of the "birth mothers" to writers conferences of that time. Like others, the Southwest Writers' Conference collected full fees from romance authors, gave them one token editor, then dedicated the rest of the workshops to poetry, journalism and various other types of writing. Since networking was virtually unknown, the only way to locate other romance authors was through such writers conferences. In the author's lonely world, editors were ethereal creatures living in the impenetrable ivory towers of New York publishing. Category romances were written exclusively by English writers for an English publisher in those days, with Janet Dailey being the first American to eventually break the barrier.

RWA had a long gestation. It took almost two years to find sixty-eight writers, the nucleus of the organization. The founders then asked editor Vivian Stephens to contact the publishing community for us, and she accepted the challenge.

On December 15, 1980, after a long and difficult labor, Romance Writers of America was born in the small meeting room of a Texas bank in northwest Houston.

The birth mothers were Rita Clay Estrada, Rita Gallagher, Parris Afton Bonds, Sondra Stanford and Peggy Cleaves (aka Ann Majors).

Along with Vivian Stephens, 36 writing midwives and 1 writing spouse attended:

Roslyn Alsobrook	Betty Henricks	Janet Prange
Irene Barthomew	Nancy Hermann	Cindy Richardson
Mary Lynn Baxter	Pat Hudgins	Nancy Riner

Lola Bellotte	Christina Jones	Joyce Saenz
Sara Bird	Kit O'Brien Jones	Glenda Sanders
Delores Blankenship	Kim Langone	Annette Sanford
Ina Bott	Susan Lowe	Linda Shaw
Sandra Brown	Janice Susan May	Barbara Stephens
Laura Castoro	Kathryn Milton	Dan Trent
Judy Crawford	Jan Minter	Lynda Trent
Mary Tate Engles	Sandra Mirines	Dorothy Weller
C. Folk	Celina Rios Mullan	Pam Zollman

On that memorable day, Rita Clay Estrada was elected first president, and the other four birth mothers became members of the first board of directors. Rita Gallagher, in addition to her post on the board of directors, became the first RWA newsletter editor and conference coordinator.

RWA was established with the following mission:

- To network and share information with others in the genre.

- To help romance authors understand the business of writing.

- To bring romance authors in contact with editors and agents.

- To give ready access to the changing tastes of readers and, ultimately, the changing marketplace.

- To give romance authors identity and a respectable voice in publishing.

Romance Writers of America became a viable entity in June 1981 during its first conference held at the Woodlands, just north of Houston, Texas. The first romance wave was cresting that summer, and 45 editors and agents paid their own way to attend. Having planned for a conference of approximately 100 to 150 people, the birth mothers and their volunteers were astonished at the overwhelming response. Along with radio and television crews from CBS, ABC and NBC, national magazine and newspaper reporters descended upon the conference center. Authors with reserved rooms had to be moved from the Woodlands Inn and placed in hotels and motels along the freeway and at the airport.

Wondering at this strange romance phenomenon bursting upon the publishing scene, university professors with invisible microscopes and lengthy questionnaires came to study romance readers as well as writers. But, like the elusive atom, romance eluded the probing search and most questions went unanswered. Yet, to romance authors and readers alike the answer was and always had been evident: Romance is an inherent part of living. A life without romance is like popcorn without butter and salt. Romance gives flavor to life, and its skilled authors whip up concoctions that are unique yet satisfying each time a book is served up for reader enjoyment.

That memorable first conference in the summer of 1981 was attended by 800 people, and the first Golden Heart Awards banquet was held before an audience of 1,200. When the conference ended, our baby was no longer an infant.

Romance Writers of America grew rapidly through the 1980s, and, in this last decade of the twentieth century, it is the largest writers organization in the world. RWA membership has reached nearly 9,000, with members in every state as well as Canada, Great Britain, Australia, New Zealand and numerous far-flung lands throughout the world.

Sondra Stanford left this earthly plane in 1991, and the four remaining founders still mourn her passing.

On that long ago day in December 1980, the initial charter members sparked a big-bang explosion. As a still-growing teenager, Romance Writers of America looks to the future with confidence, secure in the knowledge that guidance by elected leaders and dedicated members will bring each shining goal to glorious fruition.

PART 1
The Business of Romance

CHAPTER 1

Who Needs an Agent, Anyway?

Richard Curtis

Agent

Out of every fifteen thousand unsolicited manuscripts submitted by authors to any given trade book publisher, one will get selected from the slush pile and go on to get published. Maybe.

But you don't need an agent.

You think your novel is the greatest thing since *Gone With the Wind*, yet it sounds so arrogant to say that when you submit it to editors.

But you don't need an agent.

Fifty years ago an author could choose among several hundred viable trade book publishers to submit a manuscript to. Today there are seven or eight.

But you don't need an agent.

Despite the odds, you've somehow managed to sell your first book, but the publisher demands movie, television, electronic, multimedia, merchandising and translation rights and will split all proceeds with you on a fifty-fifty basis, take it or leave it.

But you don't need an agent.

You have the best editor in the world, and she's just told you she's decided to become an advertising executive. She hasn't a clue who will be your new editor, and neither do you.

But you don't need an agent.

Tomorrow is publication day of your book, but you still haven't collected the advance due on acceptance of the manuscript.

But you don't need an agent.

Foreign rights revenue on your book could double your writing income if only you knew the names of some foreign publishers.

But you don't need an agent.

Your book would make a perfect high-budget movie, only you can't get any studio story editors to answer your mail, faxes or phone calls.

But you don't need an agent.

Your publication date has been postponed twice, you hate your book jacket, the typeface is tiny, and your publisher refuses to spend a dime on publicity.

But you don't need an agent.

The announced first printing of your book was 25,000 copies; your first royalty statement reports 1,250 copies sold.

But you don't need an agent.

Unless you are capable of handling any and all of these situations, plus another fifteen or twenty I can think of off the top of my head, you'd probably be wise to rethink your decision to go it alone. I know, I know, I'm the author of a book called *How to Be Your Own Literary Agent*. Aren't I talking out of both sides of my mouth?

Well, you certainly can handle your own writing career if you're willing to invest a good deal of time and energy into it. But, as the stakes continue to get higher and the conditions tougher, the question is whether you really want to make that investment.

To help you make your decision, let me play psychiatrist and analyze why you stubbornly refuse to seek the services of a literary agent.

Most likely you're in denial. Like many people in that state of mind, you cherish an unrealistic image of what the world is like. And the image you cherish of the publishing world is one of manuscripts composed on a manual typewriter, personally submitted to a tweedy editor at an oak desk in a book-lined office; of a charming handwritten letter arriving one day informing you that your work has melted his heart and inviting you to luncheon to review your story at length and discuss the terms of a contract; of your book being lovingly designed and set in moveable type . . .

What a glorious, romantic fantasy. If only this were the 1930s, you would stand an excellent chance of realizing it.

But this is the late 1990s. We are heading for the twenty-first century, and the publishing landscape of this new age will be—already is—as unfamiliar to the average writer as the terrain of the Gobi Desert. Will you be able to traverse it without the guidance of a professional? Let's look at some topological features and see.

Because you're in denial, you probably haven't noticed that the scores of wonderful, individualistic trade book publishers that thrived earlier in our century have been reduced, through mergers, acquisitions and bankruptcies, into fewer than a dozen superpublishers operating today. If you're thinking of submitting your manuscript simultaneously to Knopf, Random House, Pantheon, Crown, Villard House, Ballantine and Del Rey, you're probably not aware that they are all divisions of the same corporation, Random House. Agents are aware of this fact, however, and if they choose to submit simultaneously to some of Random House's component publishers, they understand the protocols and proprieties. If you don't, you may be making a serious error.

Nor may you have noticed that today's trade book publishers are multinational in scope and multimedia in range. When you buy a Harper book, some of the profit will find its way into the bank account of its Australian owner; and the paycheck of the editor who acquired that Doubleday best-seller you're reading comes out of the assets of a German corporation. Even U.S. publishers who are not foreign owned are hungry for foreign revenue and aggressively negotiate for foreign rights when they acquire books. Do you know how to resist their pressure? Are you able to set a value on them if you decide to surrender them to a publisher? If you manage to reserve them, will you know what to do with them?

And what about all those electronic and multimedia rights that everybody is talking about? The most significant change in the language of book contracts in the last few years has been the addition of provisions for the adaptation of writers' work into computer-compatible media. This may not at first seem to be pertinent to your writing, and yet it is the issue over which authors organizations and publishers have been conducting fierce warfare. The winner will have the right to license adaptations and dramatizations of your novels for display on computer screens or distribution over the vast online electronic networks springing up worldwide.

Knowledgeable authors and agents are alarmed that conceding those rights to publishers jeopardizes the possibility of licensing their books to movie and television producers. Studios and networks demand the right to exploit electronic versions of the movies they make from books, and if these have been retained by publishers, it could dampen or kill the movie/television deal.

If much of this sounds like rocket science to you, or you find it incredibly boring, or you believe it's a writer's job to write and let someone else worry about this stuff, you've just presented the best possible case for hiring an agent.

But there's more. Authors in denial usually manifest severe symptoms of Maxwell Perkins Syndrome, a nostalgic longing for tweedy, paternal editors who nurture authors, lovingly pore over every word of their scripts, occupy the same desks for forty years and buy writers martinis and lunch when they're depressed. Who wouldn't want to dwell in such a heavenly fantasy world? Especially with a reality in which harassed editors scarcely have time to eat at their desks, let alone take a depressed author to lunch. They edit manuscripts off word processing disks and hop jobs every couple of years, going from one twenty-four-year-old boss to another. They've never touched tweed, let alone worn it, and don't know the difference between a martini and a Molotov cocktail.

In order to compensate for the constant turnover of editors and the destabilization of editorial functions, most agents have stepped into a far more active editorial role with their authors. Rare is the agent who simply takes what you write, submits it and collects your check. Today's agents commonly read and critique manuscripts by professional clients, even the biggest. And not a few advise their clients—again, even the biggest—to set aside the occasional stinker that every writer produces from time to time. There isn't an author in the world so objective about his or her own work.

Today's editor is a corporate animal accustomed to reaching decisions by consensus with a committee of other corporate animals and is therefore often afraid, if not completely incapable, of taking sole responsibility for the acquisition of a manuscript. That doesn't make him a bad person. In fact, editors today are as nice as anyone you'll ever meet. It's just that they work for companies whose agendas are to make large profits for their owners, and that agenda is frequently at the expense of authors. If you don't know how to penetrate the corporate mask, to be professional and businesslike with editors, you may be severely disappointed when your friendly editor tells you your publisher has cut your printing in half, given you a lousy cover or positioned your romance somewhere on the list between the *Belgian Waffle Cook Book* and the *Auto Mechanics' Repair Manual*.

Although agents, too, are on a friendly basis with most editors, they bear the scars of many a battle with them over precisely the kinds of issues I've just described. Agents understand that charming editors are employed by not-so-charming corporations. Despite warm friendships with editors, agents are constantly hassling them, advocating that bigger printing, that better cover, that better position on the list, and though they may not win every battle, they make sure that editors are mindful that someone is constantly watching over their shoulders, ready to jump in when she hears something she doesn't like. Few authors possess that combination of diplomatic tact, bravado and steely determination, but even those that do are afraid to bite the hand that feeds them.

Another way authors desperately need help is in promoting themselves. It's one thing for an agent to describe you as the finest storyteller since Charlotte Brontë but quite another for you to depict yourself that way. Do you really think anyone will believe you when you pitch your own book as the most compelling novel you've ever read? But if a top agent were to pitch it that way, I guarantee he could have any editor in the publishing industry reading your manuscript overnight. (Of course, it had better be true: Agents get to use that line once in a lifetime!)

In the final, delusional stages of the Maxwell Perkins Syndrome, authors anxiously tear open the envelopes containing their semiannual royalty statements, seeking a simple accounting of copies sold, accompanied by a handsome check. The shock to their systems when they read a scarcely comprehensible statement filled with negative numbers is often enough to drive them over the brink of madness. You can always identify such authors: They're the ones pathetically shaking empty royalty statement envelopes in the vain hope of making checks materialize out of them. Agents are experienced in reading royalty statements and detecting hidden or excessive withholding of royalties. If you're not, or can't be bothered to be, you'll one day be the owner of a prized collection of royalty statements that have a lot of minus signs on them.

When I lecture to authors groups, I ask the audience a trick question: Who is the most powerful member of a publisher's editorial board? Predictably, they answer that it's the chairman of the board, publisher or editor in chief. Remember, I said it's a trick question.

The most powerful member of a publisher's editorial board is the agent. Of course, agents don't actually sit on editorial boards. But their influence over every aspect of the publishing process— that magical word *clout*—is so enormous and pervasive that few critical decisions concerning important authors are made without taking into consideration the agents' input, to say nothing of actually soliciting it.

In his book about literary agents, my colleague Michael Larsen cites James Frey, a mystery writer. "Do you need an agent?" writes Frey. "No, you don't need an agent. You don't need a dentist, either. You can fill your own teeth."

CHAPTER 2

The Life and Times of a Manuscript

Kate Duffy

Editor, Zebra-Kensington

We're going to explore what happens when you send a manuscript to me, an editor at a major romance publishing house.

BEYOND THE SLUSH PILE

If the manuscript lands on my desk, I must presuppose that it is requested material. Either you or your agent have asked me by phone or letter if the work is something I wish to review. (An agented submission is generally regarded in a better light than an unagented one. The agent vouches for the work, and therefore the burden of proof on the writer is not as great.) You or your agent knows what kinds of books my publishing house produces, and you have targeted us as a possible home for your project. If you send me science fiction, for example, you have not done your homework. We don't publish it. If the manuscript is not sent to a specific editor, it is relegated to the slush pile and, assuming you have included postage, returned unread.

After opening whatever packing the manuscript comes in (preferably a Jiffylite mailer), I read the cover letter. The cover letter should be direct and to the point. I want to be reminded, if we have spoken about the book before, of the genre and the plot. I want to know if the manuscript is completed and, if so, what the word count is. I want to know if this is a first novel. If not, I want to see your previous publishing history. In the case of a work of nonfiction, I need to know your qualifications for writing with authority on the subject.

If I am persuaded by the cover letter, I will have an in-house reader take a look and give me a reader's report. A reader's report generally consists of one to three paragraphs of plot description and a final paragraph that is the reader's opinion. This is the point beyond which the vast majority of the manuscripts will receive no further attention. To put it plainly, my associate who reads for me is very, very difficult to please and saves me from having to read a great volume of unpublishable material.

You might be wondering what on earth I am doing if she is making all the decisions. I read option material, completed manuscripts that we own, revised manuscripts, and every once in a while, I edit. I read submissions in which I already have an interest, e.g., a *New York Times* best-seller looking for a new home, or works on a subject that has a particular appeal to me. I spend time in meetings and on the phone. I share information about acquired books with the contracts department, art department, copy department, production department and sales department. I am the liaison between the author and the publishing house, and I try to keep both parties informed about what the other is up to. There's more, but hopefully that gives you an idea of why editors do have to rely on readers.

THE DECISION TO PUBLISH

If the manuscript is recommended by the reader, I will take a look at it. If I like it, I will either present it at the editorial meeting or I will ask another editor to do a second read. This "second read" concept is a little complicated, but let me give you an example of when a second read is imperative. Nothing is acquired for hardcover publication unless the executive editor of that program supports the buy. Hers is not the only vote. I also have to convince the editor in chief, the publisher, sales and sometimes publicity, depending on the nature of the project. So in building a case for the acquisition of a title, I might want to have another editor on my side prior to the editorial meeting.

There is nothing sacred in an editorial meeting. Each time you present a book at the editorial meeting, you are trying to convince a group of professionals that this work is worthy of the time and resources of the entire company. No matter how big or small the advance, it comes down to that same thing every time. The majority of the people at the editorial meeting have not read the manuscript. So in the same way that the author has convinced me of the merit and potential of his work and has made me care about it, I have to convince others and make them care.

See what's happening here? At first, it was your book, then it was your agent's book, now I feel it's my book. I want the company to regard it as *our* book.

After the editorial meeting, it's time to do a profit and loss (P&L) statement. This is a financial forecast of the monies expected to be necessary to acquire, produce and publish the finished book and the profit or loss that will result. Most, but not all, books under consideration require this.

After the publisher and the editor in chief review the P&L, the decision is made about whether to buy the book and what terms we are prepared to offer.

Let's assume we offered an acceptable, possibly philanthropic, advance against royalties. You're thrilled, we're delighted and now we start to look for the right slot on the schedule.

THE SLOTS

We are talking about scheduling here. Numerous factors are taken into account by both mass market and category series romance publishers. But both begin with a governing mandate to deliver to the retailers a specific number of a specific type of book every month. The factors that influence scheduling a title are best explored by following the progress of a book from the time it is acquired.

Let's say I am buying a long (125,000 words) historical romance by a previously published author. To get to this point, I have had to justify to the editor in chief several concerns: We need this book because we are low in inventory, because someone has failed to deliver a book on time, because according to the P&L we can make money by publishing this title and because I see a longer partnership with this author than just this one project. At this time, we are already factoring in *when* and *where*—which translates into which month and in what position on the schedule the book will be published. Nothing is engraved in stone, but certain realities are acknowledged that will influence the scheduling of this title.

So when I acquire the book, it will either go into inventory or it will be tentatively scheduled. Looking at the delivery date of the completed manuscript and availability of the right slot, I claim a place on the schedule for this book, knowing that it will likely move. I look at the schedule to see what (at this time) we think we will be publishing in that same month. I ask myself questions like: Is there a problem with the title? Do we have a book with the same location and time frame already scheduled? If the author writes for another house, when is it publishing? When was the author last published? Does this author usually meet the deadline agreed to in the contract for delivery of the manuscript?

One thing I should point out is that because of the lead time needed to get material and information about all the books we are publishing to other departments, little by little the schedule does start to be engraved in stone. Schedule changes are made all the time, of course. But there is a ripple effect that can be minimized the farther ahead you know about any circumstance that will affect, say, the delivery of a completed manuscript. I have had authors call and tell me that their books will be two weeks or so late. That did not affect the schedule. I am currently waiting for a book that is eight months late. Needless to say, I am not holding my breath, nor am I holding a space for this title on any schedule. This does have an impact on sales as the length of time between books on sale is prolonged. These consequences will be dealt with by the author and my publishing house if and when hell freezes over, pigs fly and this book is delivered.

Back to the hypothetical. The book is delivered. It needs revisions. I may feel there is not enough time if the book stays where it is currently scheduled, so I look to find another slot. The schedule is juggled, and the book is rescheduled, or "bumped." The departments that have to be informed of these changes are notified. Only when the manuscript is accepted and all of that month's titles have been reviewed at a marketing meeting do I start to feel safe.

A note about bumping: Many authors feel unhappy when their books are bumped, as if it were something personal. Not at all. Books are rescheduled for any number of reasons. Sometimes we can explain it to an author's satisfaction, but not always.

Every book we buy presents its own set of challenges when it comes to scheduling. When I worked in category series romance publishing, for example, our scheduling focused a great deal on the content of the book. We didn't want to duplicate names, occupations, locations or competing publications by the same author. From anthologies that are tied into particular events, like a Christmas collection, to a reprint from a hardcover house that we contractually have to publish within a certain time frame, we are back to the reality of twelve months in a year and a particular number of slots dedicated to a particular type of book for each one of those months.

You may have noticed that I haven't touched on the fact that we consider the amount of money we paid to the author as an advance against royalties. Clearly, we want to recoup costs and see a profit from this venture. The position of the book on the schedule reflects what quantities we will want to distribute to have the best possible chance of being successful. This is a marketing decision best made by people who can see "the big picture." The books that we love, the books that you write and I read, those books that we know deserve a wider readership have to be viewed dispassionately. And so, sometimes at a marketing meeting, the schedule will be juggled again to reflect the input of the sales department and the judgment of the publisher.

FROM MANUSCRIPT TO BOUND BOOK

Once a schedule for publication is established, there are deadlines to be met by every person connected with the publication and distribution of the book.

I am given a date by which the production department must receive the edited manuscript so that they can give it to a copyeditor. My editing usually addresses plot, characterization and voice. I am the first reader, and I get to share any concerns I have about the manuscript with the author. For example: If there is a scene that shows a character doing or saying something that just doesn't ring true to me, I discuss it with the author. If I can't convince the author of the validity of my point, the scene stays as written.

When the author and I are happy with the book, we entrust it to a copyeditor. The copyeditor checks for grammar, style and punctuation. He will also flag anything he doesn't understand, like a possible anachronism or something he thinks the author and editor might have missed.

An art fact sheet is prepared for the art department describing the book and suggesting possible approaches. An artist is commissioned and given a delivery date for the cover art: first a sketch, and when the sketch is approved, the finished art, which still may need to be revised.

A copy of the manuscript and any other relevant materials (synopsis, quotes, previous covers) go to the copy department so they can produce jacket copy. The subsidiary rights department might need a copy of the manuscript as well.

Publicity can send out manuscripts, page proofs or bound galleys (aka advance reading copies) for review by various trade publications.

Sales solicits orders for the book. A print order is set, and the book is printed, bound and distributed.

That's pretty much it. Piece of cake. Oh, last year approximately five hundred titles were published by us. And each one went through this process.

CHAPTER 3

Between Publisher and Bookstore

Sandy Jaffe

Distributor

To many authors wholesalers are, alternately, either saviors or "the scum of the earth." How can we be both, you ask? Maybe it's because many authors don't completely understand how the distribution process works. I firmly believe that as an author you should understand all facets of this industry to best utilize available resources and get the most "bang" for your buck/book! Keeping that goal in mind, I'll attempt to explain how the distribution process works.

WHY DO BOOKSTORES USE A WHOLESALER?

Wholesalers are the bookseller's best friend. Maintaining just-in-time inventory, being able to bank on fast delivery of hot product and having the latest, up-to-the-minute selling strategies are just a few of the advantages that bookstores serviced regularly by their regional wholesalers enjoy.

A typical bookstore needs every inch of its space to be user-friendly for its customers. Whether filled to the gills with titles or sharing leisurely café space and reading nooks, not many stores can afford a back room for extra inventory—nor should they. Books are big business in the 1990s, and competition is stiff. There is almost always another bookstore just a short distance away. Selling space, more books per inch, must always be a primary consideration. Even the relaxing reading space conducive to the Sunday browser must be designed for maximum marketing potential. These priorities have made the back room obsolete and the wholesaler who can deliver inventory fast a necessity.

A good regional wholesaler carrying best-sellers, a strong back-list and some midlist, together with a few specialty genres, such as romance, science fiction and juvenile, can support bookstores and eliminate their need to carry any more than "selling" inventory. Working on the basic eighty-twenty premise that 80 percent of sales comes from 20 percent of inventory, wholesalers are an essential part of a successful marketing plan.

Fast delivery is an absolute necessity for the wholesaler, which is why the really good ones generally have well-defined geographic markets that they cover exclusively. A midwest wholesaler in St. Louis, for example, would likely sell mainly in the central corridor of the United States, where her customers could plan on next- or second-day delivery. This way stores can order two or three times a week and maintain inventory that is selling without having to over-order to protect themselves against the competition.

Fast delivery also ensures that a hot product is available when you need it. Best-sellers need to be in bookstores constantly because a customer who wants the latest Danielle Steel novel won't buy the Tom Clancy instead. It is unlike almost all other retail, where a suitable beige sweater may exist in several forms. In the book world, that customer in search of Danielle Steel will likely leave the first store and head for another. Alas, the sale is lost and so, maybe, is the customer when "next time" comes. A wholesaler who can get the stores the books they need when they need them is essential.

There are also wholesalers who offer special programs geared toward the small independent bookstores, selling to them directly. For stores too small to see most publishers, buying direct from a wholesaler who provides a catalog with descriptions of key titles can be a real benefit. It is an opportunity to avoid high publisher minimums but still get new releases in the same timely way. Wholesalers generally receive titles enough in advance of laydown dates (preestablished release dates upon which booksellers may begin selling specified books) to provide bookstores in their regions with the same delivery date the publishers do. There are even wholesalers who, because of their buying and selling expertise, sell directly to customers outside their traditional geographic areas. This works well mainly with chains that have a centralized buying office and stores in a wide variety of locales. The advantages to them of buying direct from a wholesaler, as opposed to the publisher, are varied. While they do give up a point or two in discount, often they still realize a cost savings with the ability to minimize accounting, consolidate returns and, most especially, to buy from multiple publishers at one time. It is easier to manage a budget when several publishers are presented at once because the buyer doesn't have to worry about holding out too many or too few dollars for another publisher's list.

Wholesalers who offer these specialized services are supporting booksellers in the most critical way, saving them time and money. Additionally, the information a wholesaler can provide regarding sales trends on a particular series or author can be invaluable. The midwest wholesale buyer knows, for example, how an author's sales are growing or dropping in, say, Chicago vs. Texas because many different markets are represented with each regional wholesaler. This information in advance of a buy can help protect the bookseller from costly mistakes.

The wholesalers' main commodity is always information, not only when it is a specialized program they are selling, but also in the course of their regular business. The telephone sales force of the wholesaler is a priceless source of the stream of information booksellers need to stay current and increase sales. A quick phone call can yield publicity information such as whose book is being featured on *Oprah* or whose radio program is interviewing which author. These kinds of advance tips enable a store to have plenty of stock when the customers start calling. A bookseller can be proactive instead of reactive. Sales are saved because again, with increasingly tough competition in almost every market, customers' loyalty is only as strong as the store's stock.

The telephone salespeople at a wholesaler are also usually the first people to spot important selling trends. Their Monday morning calls to a variety of kinds of bookstores in a broad gamut of markets gives them a good picture of weekend sales around the country. They are often able to spot potential best-sellers weeks before they actually hit the list. They can also create a big seller because their hand-selling touches so many different markets. A telephone sales-person who's well informed and has a good reputation in the book industry can make a real difference in the success of a title. This can create sales for booksellers whose enthusiasm gets tweaked with timely, accurate information.

Wholesalers also can provide signed copies of books to stores that normally might not be able to access a particular author. This too can yield increased sales. Some small stores have created a special niche selling signed copies of books that are supplied by wholesalers. They can maintain a diversified stock of authors and titles by using several wholesalers who generally will have different authors represented among their signed stock, since author tours generally include a broad range of tour cities.

Since the book industry has become such a hot arena, with competition increasing daily, booksellers have had to become savvy businesspeople. The image of the person sitting behind the counter reading and chatting about great literature has given way to espresso bars, dessert cafés, discounted best-sellers and high-tech computer centers. With everyone looking for an edge, the partnership between booksellers and wholesalers is important to the survival and success of the industry.

THE ROLE OF THE DEMAND JOBBER

A demand jobber fulfills its customers', the bookstores', orders, or "demands," for books but does not have established outlets at which they may "force" or place books. Thus, the demand jobber's primary goal is to get the title information to its customer base, making it convenient and enticing for those bookstores to place orders. We utilize several methods to impart this information: monthly advance/ preview catalog, sell-sheets, publisher teaser samplers, telemarketing, mailing of lists of newly received titles, microfiche, library mailings, warehouse shopping and book displays at trade shows, among others. Next you ask, "How does my book get listed in any or all of these vehicles?" That begins with your book being purchased by the wholesaler from the publisher.

PURCHASING THE BOOK

Most buyers see sales reps for each of the key mass market publishers on a monthly basis, approximately three to four months prior to the publication months, e.g., February's new releases, which ship in January, are bought in October. Before the scheduled sales appointment, the buyer will have been provided with a publisher's kit, which contains covers, catalogs and any publisher-driven selling pieces. As you can see, the initial demand for a title is generated by the publisher.

The buyer will then make selections from each publisher each month, based upon many criteria, including but not limited to: the author's previous track record; the subgenre's (e.g., historical, futuristic, contemporary or time travel) performance/viability; whether the title is a new release or a reissue; the publisher's track record and promotional machine; the title's positioning on the publisher's list that month; the cover treatment (of particular interest in midlist titles); how many vehicles the wholesaler can use to sell it or markets the wholesaler can approach; whether it's part of a series or a stand-alone novel; the author's hometown (again, more important on midlist titles); any information from the author on what she is planning regarding promotion and publicity; and the sales rep's input (he might know how an author sells into a particular region that might be a new territory for the wholesaler, or he might be privy to a publisher's or author's plans that are not apparent in the kit material). Once a wholesaler has bought the book, it then proceeds to the marketing stages.

MARKETING

Most demand jobbers/wholesalers produce some version of an annotated monthly new releases advance catalog or newsletter, with order forms, of course. These catalogs vary in publication time, with some arriving in the store or library as early as six weeks prior to the books' release from the publishers and others arriving as late as two weeks after the new titles are released. These catalogs vary in size, format and content. Some consist of a few pages of listings by category, and/or publisher as part of a monthly newsletter with reviews of key titles. Others are arranged by publisher, with annotations for each title. Still others are arranged by category, with annotations (and sometimes pictures) per title. Some list every title purchased for that month. Others only list the first and second tiers of the lists. Other catalogs list all new titles but not reissues. Some wholesalers do separate catalogs for mass market and trade and hardcover titles, while other publishers combine them all into one catalog. Most of these vehicles allow and actually encourage space for publishers' advertisements since it helps defray the cost of the catalog. Many wholesalers will also accept ads from authors, if the prepared ads meet their catalogs' specifications.

In addition to the aforementioned catalogs, many wholesalers also do regular mailings to their accounts. These may include, but again are not necessarily limited to, thematic flyers, e.g., romance for Valentine's Day; lists of new titles arriving in stores in a particular week; publisher-driven promotions, e.g., Harper Monogram's 101 Days of Romance; publisher teaser samplers; flyers designed by authors; microfiche and topical catalogs. These are additional marketing tools to get titles in front of the bookstore manager or librarian and ultimately into the hand of the romance reader.

THE AUTHOR'S ROLE IN MARKETING

Keep in mind that the above are marketing tools to the trade only and need to be reinforced by the author with her promotions and publicity. The author's support and enthusiasm for her title is a necessary component for the *total* marketing plan; all other vehicles could be for naught unless the author is willing to promote her title as well. You can utilize your local wholesalers/jobbers as part of these plans by visiting their distribution centers once your books have arrived and signing and stickering all of their stock. They can then use this as a telemarketing tool to their customers and make some bookstore managers very happy. If the wholesalers produce catalogs or mailings, get their rate sheets and see about advertising in them, or provide them with teaser samplers (if your publisher did one for your title). You could also do your own professional-looking flyer with cover art and excerpts, for example.

Remember, the wholesale buyers must first purchase the book to set all the wheels in motion, so make sure you notify them of your title three to four months prior to its publication date. Something in writing works best; they can then keep it with the publisher kit so it's right in front of them when it's time to do the buy from that publisher. Learn the names of the advertising managers at your local wholesalers. This way, if you plan to piggyback on some of their promotions but you can't reach the buyer, you can call the advertising manager to get dates for deadlines, ad rate sheets, etc.

If you are not adept at planning promotions, ask the wholesale buyers or advertising managers to lunch or schedule a meeting. See if you can do some collective brainstorming for promotional ideas.

Sometimes two or three heads *can* be better than one.

Once your book has been shipped from the publisher and you are starting your publicity, please keep your wholesalers apprised of any key details. Will your book be featured in a local newspaper or on a radio show? Have you been asked to do any signings? Please let the buyer know these details so that he can then have the telemarketing staff share this information with bookstores and, hopefully, increase the sale of your title. Nothing will catch the attention of a store manager more than upcoming publicity.

Also, many wholesaler buyers work closely with the local Romance Writers of America chapter, oftentimes participating in local panel discussions or seminars. If you are a member and are able to attend these functions, please come prepared with things like jacket covers, business cards and flyers to give to the buyers. Again, these are marketing tools they can share with their customers, thereby increasing sales for everyone involved.

Remember that the wholesaler makes your title available to hundreds of outlets, both in the United States and overseas. The distribution channels and systems can benefit you greatly, especially if you take advantage of the special opportunities offered to your title by the wholesale process and marketing tools.

CHAPTER 4

How to Handle Publicity

Joan Schulhafer

Publicist

Publicity plays an important role for trade publishers. Along with advertising and promotion, it helps not only to sell books to consumers, but aids in getting the books into stores initially.

PUBLICITY VS. ADVERTISING AND PROMOTION

Many people confuse the roles of publicity, advertising and promotion, and the language can be confusing. Terms like *self-promotion* aren't easy to define. Does it mean promotion in the sense of point-of-purchase promotional materials? Does it mean authors promoting themselves as personalities? Or does it mean authors promoting specific books on their own? Defining *publicity*, *advertising* and *promotion* seems to depend on the context in which the words are used and the environment the speaker is in. For example, at a romance writers conference, *self-promotion* is a blanket term covering publicity, advertising *and* promotion; however, for most publishers, those three terms define specific programs and functions that work hand in hand and often overlap.

Advertising is rather straightforward in the sense of purchasing advertising space. Of course, actually creating the campaign and the ads themselves is far from straightforward and involves a great deal of skill, knowledge and creativity. These attributes are an important part of deciding whether advertising is the best choice for a book's campaign. Where will the ads be most effective? What are the best images to use? What copy will best sell the book? Advertising ranges from trade advertising in publishing publications, such as *Publishers Weekly, Magazine & Bookseller* and *American Bookseller*, to ads in places such as brochures or program booklets created to serve related publishing organizations, such as the Romance Writers of America, American Booksellers Association (ABA) or the American Library Association, at events as diverse as dinners, trade shows and conventions. Consumer advertising covers everything from newsletter ads to national television campaigns. Publishers spend advertising dollars in a variety of ways, but most efforts are focused by title, not as corporate advertising.

Promotion is harder to put labels on. It can be the table at a regional ABA convention, a food fair or an outdoor festival, or the belly band around an advance copy of a book going to book buyers. It is everything that goes into the solicitation kit used by sales representatives to sell the publisher's list to buyers. It's advance information sheets, brochures, catalogs, shelf talkers, counter and floor displays, contests and items such as T-shirts, balloons and bookmarks.

Publicity is "free." It is space in print or broadcast and cable time that is not paid for. In that respect, it is believed to carry more credibility in the minds of consumers as, unlike advertising and promotion, it is not a controlled message. It is perceived as earning the coverage because of its value and interest to the audience, not because it has been purchased. Publicity can be personal appearances and lectures arranged for the purpose of selling books. It is everything from print listings of books in "round-ups" and announcement listings, to major coverage on national television. It's press kits, press releases, "pub" cards, pitch letters, tidbits for gossip columns and interviews on television, radio, cable and in print. It's bookstore or other retail signings and readings, meetings with key buyers and appearances at trade and consumer shows, conferences and conventions. It is not easy to get, and it is not easy to make it effective.

WILL *YOUR* BOOK BE PUBLICIZED?

Authors interested in publicizing their books should first get in touch with their editors to find out what plans are being made for the book. This should happen at least nine months ahead of publication so any ideas or projects to be undertaken by the author can be considered and incorporated into the plans for the books. Many publishing houses ask authors to communicate with the publicity department through their editors up until the time publicity projects commence. Authors should provide editors with the following information, if available:

- lecture schedule and anticipated travel

- specific publicity suggestions

- a listing of the author's existing media contacts with addresses

- a biography

- upcoming author-initiated signing or other publicity efforts

- past publicity history, including selected video- and audiotapes and copies of press clippings

Not every title at a publisher receives publicity attention, although review copy mailings to appropriate media are usually a standard procedure. Also, titles are brought to the attention of the media through a variety of other ways, including catalogs, listings and articles in trade publications, and conversations. It is unlikely that a publisher will pursue interviews or local publicity on every book it publishes. Not only are publishers limited by budget and the amount of staff available, the hard truth is that it just doesn't make sense to pursue publicity for every title. There's publicity, and there's effective publicity. Not every campaign will sell books, and not every author can sell his books through the media. Most publishers will try to maximize publicity opportunities for their authors; however, the publisher's viewpoint about which efforts are meaningful do not always correspond with that of the author.

It's important to understand the reality of placing a story. Most interview outlets are not interested in fiction. Unless there is a strong local tie or a newsworthy "hook" to the story being placed, more often than not the automatic answer to an interview regarding fiction is no. That no becomes even more emphatic when the work of fiction under discussion is being published as a paperback original or reprint. Believe it or not, being published is not enough. Being a best-selling author is not enough.

Take that less than welcoming environment and mix it with a shrinking media market, and the result is a major publicity challenge. True, cable is opening up many new avenues, as is the Internet, and opportunities for exposure in "niche" programming and forums have been most welcomed. However, even many of these do not yet reach significant audiences. Opportunities in local market media have suffered the most in recent years. Not so very long ago, an author could tour several cities and have a respectable or outstanding interview schedule in each location. Most cities had at least one or two local interview programs on television, a half dozen or more radio talk shows, several noon and early evening newscasts with feature interview segments and one or two daily papers.

Today, with the proliferation of syndicated television, many cities don't even have a locally produced talk/interview show. Local talk radio follows the same route, with drive time holding strong but the majority of the talk schedule originating elsewhere. There's less feature reporting on the existing newscasts, unless there's a strong local angle or event, and a lot of their interviews are tied to their public affairs requirements. Very few cities have more than one daily newspaper anymore, and the cost of paper means space is even more limited for nonessential stories.

Yet, this shrinking media market does not mean there are not opportunities for exposure. Authors should share their publicity ideas with their publishers to determine what can and cannot be done by the publicity departments. Then, if their decision is to supplement the publishers' efforts, authors should make plans well ahead of time and let their editors know what they'll be doing. The effectiveness of their efforts will be greatly enhanced by keeping the sales force informed.

THE ALL-IMPORTANT INTERVIEW

Regardless of whether the moment of truth—the interview—comes through the author's efforts or the publisher's, whether it's local or national, preparedness is the key to success. Getting publicity is one thing, handling publicity is another. It is essential for interviewees to give thought to the situation about to be entered, to try to turn it to their best advantage, and to be prepared for a variety of circumstances—in other words, to handle publicity effectively.

Preparation

Anyone anticipating media coverage should pay attention to newspaper interviews and interview programs on television and radio. The first step is to listen and read for pleasure and information, the same way writers enjoy books before deciding to write. Then it's time to listen and read for content, approach, style and delivery. Listen to the interviewers and guests, and analyze print coverage. Who's interesting and why? Do the stories contain the traditional who, what, when, where and why elements? How do the subjects use the answers to those questions to position their responses and sell themselves or their products? Since familiarity is a powerful tool in the interview environment, it is helpful to find out as much as possible about the program or publication. For instance:

- What is the program's format?

- Who is the host?

- Will the guest be speaking to the interviewer in person or via satellite or phone? If via satellite, will there be a monitor in the studio?

- What kind of guests are usually on the program, or what kind of articles does the interviewer usually write?

- In what section of the paper will the article appear?

- How long is the interview?

- Is it tape or live?

- How long is the finished interview?

- If tape or print, when will it run?

- Are others being interviewed at the same time? As a panel or in separate interviews?

Another way to prepare for interviews is to create two lists. One should be the ten most common, inoffensive questions asked, or likely to be asked. The other should be the ten toughest, most difficult questions that may be asked—regardless of whether they've ever been asked. Guests must be prepared to answer all of these questions, be able to answer them with reasonably short, concise answers and be prepared with short "sound bites" and longer, interesting or humorous anecdotes to follow up these answers.

Guests should watch what other people wear on television and in newspaper photos to decide what looks best and what will be most effective for their own interviews. Appearance shouldn't be neglected, even if the interview is not for television. Keep hair away from the face. Bright or deep colors are great for clothes (unless the program is *Face the Nation*, in which case a navy blue pin-striped suit and a light blue blouse are in order). Red is a favorite television color. Prints should be avoided. White, small stripes and small prints are a no for television. Jewelry should be unobtrusive. Dangling earrings and highly reflective earrings should be avoided. Necklines shouldn't be too low. Makeup is a plus, and even men should consider it for television.

It's important to know how to sit on television. A leg crossed in the wrong direction can mean a view of the sole of a shoe for the audience. Elbows should be kept off tables.

Authors should always bring a copy of their books with them, even onto the set, to be sure one is available.

The Dynamics of the Interview

Understanding the dynamics of the interview situation is also an important tool. Just as each guest on the air or in print has an agenda of information he wants to get across through the media, each interviewer has her own agenda—messages about herself and about the person or subject with which they are dealing.

Most interviewers want their audiences to like them, to feel comfortable with them. They work on those aspects of their personas that will accomplish this. They want their audiences to relate to them as someone liked and respected. They want to be welcomed into their audiences' homes again and again.

A lot hinges on appearance, particularly for television. Interviewers are a bit glamorous—well groomed, nicely dressed, attractively made up, wearing a great smile—and they are usually nonthreatening in their appearance. On-air talents let their audiences get to know them, perhaps inserting bits of their own backgrounds, and certainly their own opinions, into interviews. They are also attempting to entertain while they inform their audience. It is an important part of the interview, and some will do it at the expense of the guest.

In a nonconfrontational, general interview, guests can anticipate interviewers' goals as

- creating and sharing excitement and enthusiasm about a subject and bringing new information to their audiences

- showing they are enjoying the topic and that the audience should be, too

- asking the questions their audiences would ask if given the opportunity

Guests have goals, too, such as:

- creating and sharing excitement and enthusiasm about their subjects and bringing new information to the audience

- showing they are enjoying the topic and that the audience should be, too

- steering the interview toward the messages and ideas they believe their audiences most want to hear

When structuring messages for the media, it is important to put that message into the context of what the audience will want to hear. A lot that is interesting and exciting to the guest may be too specialized for an audience that's not actively involved in the same field. Some topics just aren't titillating, sexy, fun or informative for an audience that doesn't already know and care about the subject.

The Interview Scenario

That said, interviewers rely on their guests. Guests must be prepared with the main points they want to get across. The interviewers rely upon press materials and information from their research staff, if they have one, in preparing for the interview. The unfortunate situation they must always be prepared for is that some subjects don't know what they want to say beyond their initial "pitch"—their new book, movie or public affairs message.

Ideally, the interviewer views part of his responsibility as making the guest comfortable. Part of that can be to let the guest get her pitch out at the beginning of the interview so she can relax and not worry so much about getting her message across.

A good interviewer will

- take care of basic introductory questions right away to bring the audience "up to speed" on the topic being discussed

- reach for unusual questions or pursue an angle that he knows is more interesting to the audience than the basic pitch

- move quickly to audience participation, phone-ins or demonstrations if they're part of the format

An interviewer can't do these things well if he's not prepared. That means making sure he has good information to rely upon when formulating the interview, and that is the responsibility of the person arranging the interview.

Most journalists and hosts have been caught in a number of trying situations. Some guests are just bad at interviews. Some "freeze," others only want to keep reciting their sales pitches, and others have been oversold to the show or publication and should never have been put forward for an interview. It is up to the person being interviewed to be prepared and to get her message out in a way that will work for all concerned.

People being interviewed must determine what they are trying to accomplish by being interviewed and what image they are attempting to project. One way of doing this is to focus on two top priority messages and be prepared to present those messages in a minimum of time. Then the messages can be enlarged upon, as time allows, by preparing in advance. Secondary messages should be explored, prepared and used to expand and reinforce the two main messages.

It becomes clear to a guest early during an interview whether he is with a good interviewer who leads the conversation, is enthusiastic and allows him to reinforce his message; with a bad interviewer who needs the guest to take control of the situation and lead the conversation; or with an interviewer somewhere in between, not a terrible place, but less predictable than the other two.

Novelists will rarely find themselves in a confrontational, hard-hitting interview situation, although writers must be aware of this type of interview. Writers of romance, in particular, must be aware of the "young Turk" interviewer, working the feature beat but trying to make her mark on the world of journalism by uncovering a sinister underside to this popular genre.

Regardless of the type of situation a guest is in, she must work to keep the interviewer and his agenda from getting in the way of her own relationship to the audience. The final outcome the guest is seeking is a positive message to the audience, or at least that part of the audience receptive to her message.

It's important to remember that there are three people involved in each interview situation: the interviewer, the guest and the audience. That means there are three relationships involved: the interviewer-guest, interviewer-audience, and guest-audience. How the audience perceives the guest and assimilates his information should be the guest's priority, not his relationship with the interviewer.

Most interviewers' success and security depend on likability, consistent quality and a positive, ongoing relationship with the audience. Most good interviewers will assume a position secondary to that of the audience-guest relationship. There is security for them in the fact that it is their venue, and they can be expansive about letting a guest look good. Good journalists or hosts will work for an effective audience-guest relationship because that's what makes for a good interview and good interviews are what keep them on the air.

During the interview, it's important that the guest picks up on the interviewer's last question or statements to segue into the planned message or "pitch." In the case of an inappropriate question, that doesn't mean the guest has to answer the question—at least not the way the interviewer may be hoping she will.

TIPS FOR INTERVIEWEES:
- Don't be afraid to use hands when speaking, just not to excess.
- Keep your hands away from your face.
- Smile as much as is appropriate.

For example, romance novelists are often asked about sex. The question "Aren't these books all about sex?" doesn't have to be answered yes or no. A guest might answer, "Romance writers are often asked about sex. That is sometimes surprising to me since I believe love is the most important message we're giving our readers."

The interviewer may drop the question or come back to it again, and the guest must be prepared for another question along the same line. She may steer away from it, attempting to change the topic, or answer it with an anecdote. One author tells a wonderful story about being pleased to have her own children learn about sex while reading romance since the context is love and commitment, unlike so many other messages about sex that are received by young people.

A guest might also choose to have fun with this sort of question. The author of a historical romance might answer in the context of her book, posing questions such as "How did they ever get any privacy with all those snoopy people around the palace?" or "Wouldn't you prefer he had taken a bath first after he came back from battle?"

In any interview situation, it is also a good idea for the guest to involve the interviewer and make him part of what is being talked about. Asked where she gets her ideas, a guest might answer, "Well, from all around me. Right now, I'm thinking you would make an excellent romance hero."

A guest does not have to answer every question. She can also disagree with an interviewer, but it's important not to be defensive while doing so. A guest can also refuse to be a guest and simply turn down any interviews that may be problematic. However, there are no guarantees, even in well-researched situations, and the best bet is to be prepared for the best and the worst scenarios.

After an interview, interviewees should critique their "performances." They should get video- and audiotapes and clippings whenever possible and assess how effective the interviews were and how they can improve their interview skills for the future.

Lastly, guests should remember three things: (1) they can always choose not to pursue publicity; (2) they must always assume the camera or microphone is on the entire time they are in the studio; and (3) nothing, but nothing, is ever "off the record."

CHAPTER 5

The Importance of Networking

Janis Reams Hudson

RWA President

Networking—it's not just for television anymore. Nor is it still reserved solely for "the good ol' boys." Today networking is a vital tool in any business and is particularly important for writers. For the uninitiated, *networking* is the exchange of information and/or services. There are as many different reasons to reach beyond the solitary confines of your office to network with others as there are writers.

Networking doesn't happen on its own. It doesn't come along and sit down beside you at your desk, eager to tell you things you need to know. It's not a passive activity, but one you have to make happen.

Before we go any farther, I feel compelled to issue a cautionary note: Networking is not the same as gossiping. By definition, "To gossip" is to reveal personal, intimate or sensational facts or rumors about others; or to engage in 'chatty talk.' Gossiping has nothing to do with networking. The difference is important, both to your success and to your reputation. In this chapter, I'll guide you through the whys, hows and rules of networking.

"Rules? Networking sounds like a lot of bother," you say.

Ah, but the benefits, regardless of the stage of your career— from beginning writer to *New York Times* best-selling author—can prove invaluable. Before we get to the hows and rules, let's take a look at why writers should network.

WHY NETWORK

Beginning writers can learn better writing techniques by talking to other writers, finding out how they tackle a particular problem and which how-to books helped them the most, or the least. You can learn from others which publishers are looking for the type of story you're writing. You will learn, one way or another, that most publishers are compelled, for marketing reasons, to put a label on your manuscript. Since you're reading this particular book, that label is most likely to be "romance."

But your manuscript starts in 1776 and follows one family through to the year 2000. Do you know it's called a saga? Do you know which houses will not buy a saga? Networking with other writers can save you a great deal of time and effort by helping you direct your project to the proper publisher.

Research is another reason to network. Nearly all writers did something else with their time before they began writing. Regular contact with other writers can lead you to resources you might not find on your own. Maybe the writer sitting next to you at a conference is a former police officer, and you need to know something about police procedure you haven't been able to find in a book and are just too shy to call your local precinct. Or maybe that person next to you knows someone who recently had her hands on the very reference book you need and can help you track down the title.

Are you getting the idea?

Story help can also be acquired through networking. Exchanging ideas with other writers is a good way to find all the holes you've left in your plot. (Better find them now, before an editor does!) Sometimes, networking peers make terrific sounding boards and critique partners. Many experienced authors frequently reach out to each other in search of a trustworthy sounding board.

By the time you finish reading this book, you should understand that the first priority of any author is to write the very best book possible. But a career as an author does not stop there; a good book is only the beginning. The publishing business is unlike any other business animal you've ever dealt with. Networking can possibly save you from serious mistakes and help you avoid the pitfalls that have trapped many an unwary author. How so? Read on.

When an editor calls wanting to buy your book (the call will come via your agent if you have one), how do you know the offer is a fair one if you've never talked to other authors about what to expect? An offer of five thousand dollars might sound insulting if you've just heard on the news how many millions Steven King received on his new contract.

This is where networking can help you keep your feet on the ground. Steven King's multimillion-dollar advance made the news because it was just that—news. Something extraordinary.

If the editor offers you 4 percent royalties, networking with other authors *in advance of getting the offer* will tell you that few houses still offer such a low rate to a romance author, even a first-time author.

Are you getting the picture?

Through networking, you can learn which clauses in the contract are usually negotiable and which are usually not; which agents like to edit your manuscript and which don't; which editors like to rewrite your work and which don't. You can learn how books get distributed, which booksellers are romance-author friendly, which bookstores advertise upcoming autographings and which ones just stick the author at a table and walk away.

A word about agents and the benefits of networking: My personal preference is to have an agent working for me. But a bad or unscrupulous agent (yes, they do exist) is worse than having no agent at all. Agents work for you, not the other way around. Just as you would check the references of any employee you were considering hiring, check out an agent before agreeing to hire him. For this, there is nothing like personal contact—networking—with those who have worked with that agent.

A good network of authors can also keep you abreast of the current market. Even if you have an agent, it's still *your* career, so you have to pay attention. Sending your time-travel romance to an editor who hates time travel will not only slow down the assumed eventual sale of your manuscript, but will tell that editor that you didn't do your homework or you would have known not to waste your postage and her time.

Even above all of the legitimate business reasons to reach out to others in your field and network, there is one thing aside from business concerns that is perhaps the most important reason to network with other authors, specifically, authors of your own genre: to save your sanity.

No, I'm not joking. Writing is of necessity a solitary endeavor.

It's just you and the words you sometimes have to pull from your mind and heart with steel pliers. Just you and the story. Sometimes the story won't go well. Sometimes your nonwriter family and friends will not take your very real concerns about a character, a plot, a contract seriously. Sometimes you just can't face that blank screen or blank sheet of paper.

This is when your network of author friends becomes more than a network, more than moral support. They become your lifeline. No one understands what a writer goes through, the fears, the uncertainty, sometimes the envy or downright jealousy of another's success or even the tremendous high over a scene that goes well, like another writer. Especially another writer you've built a relationship with over time by networking. When things don't go well, you need to talk it out with people you trust, people who experience the same frustrations and disappointments, the same hopes and dreams as you. When things do go well, you need to celebrate with someone who understands why you're so excited.

With time, you'll come to relate differently with different networking partners. I have one writer I call when I need to be reminded of the real world because she does not let writing consume her life the way I do. I call another when I'm in the mood to whine because she doesn't scoff at my whining. A third I call when I need a good swift kick in the pants to get me going on a story because she's a genius at picking out the problem and pointing to solutions. I may not use her solutions, but she jump-starts my mind.

There is, of course, a reverse side to networking. It cannot be all taking on your part. You have to give, too. My networking partners call me when they need to. Giving can sometimes be as helpful, as inspiring, as rejuvenating as receiving.

How does it all work? Following are some ways to start.

HOW TO NETWORK

To network, you must be in contact with other writers. This is not as difficult as it might sound to those of you who don't know any other writers.

First, Romance Writers of America has more than 150 local chapters around the world: one in Australia, the rest in the United States and Canada. There's also an electronic chapter, RWA Online, on CompuServe, and Outreach International Romance Writers

Chapter, which meets "by mail" via its newsletter and is open to all RWA members. Many local chapters hold annual conferences and workshops where you can meet other romance writers. Membership in national RWA is required to join a chapter, but most chapters allow a writer to visit a couple of times before requiring you to join.

National RWA, then, becomes your key source for networking. Members receive a monthly magazine and access to local chapters and the national annual conference, held in a different city each year, where we gather to network with other writers, agents and editors, attend educational workshops and honor the best among us with our annual RITA Awards Ceremony.

But there are network sources other than RWA. There are other genre writing organizations if your interests stretch beyond romance. Most large cities have local writers organizations that are non-genre specific. Writing workshops and conferences are common, too. Check with your library or university.

Magazines such as *Writer's Digest*, *The Writer*, *Romantic Times* and *Affaire de Coeur* can also help get you on the road to networking. Every writer should subscribe to *Publishers Weekly*.

The hottest networking tool these days is the World Wide Web on the Internet. Homepages for writers are springing up every day. In addition, nearly every research topic a writer could need is covered on the Web. Besides the Web, there are writers' topics on all of the major electronic bulletin board services such as America OnLine, CompuServe, Prodigy and GEnie. Electronic networking is the wave of the future.

Still, nothing can beat the personal touch. At conferences and workshops, make it a point to introduce yourself to people. Find writers with like interests, or at the same career level as you, and exchange addresses and phone numbers. Keep in touch with each other. Take an interest in each other. Six months down the road you're likely to discover that the last person you met on your way home from the conference has a third cousin who teaches ballet, and you need to know what a plié is for your ballerina heroine. And you might discover that all the organic knowledge you cultivated during your Earth Mother years is not going to waste now that you eat regularly from cans and frozen cartons; your new writer friend could really use some of your information for her book.

Give and take. Back and forth.

At conferences you'll meet agents and editors. A short note

afterward stating that you enjoyed meeting them might help get your manuscript read more quickly than someone else's when you query them a year later. You never know. (Agents, and particularly editors, have memories like elephants.)

GOLDEN RULES OF NETWORKING

Rules? Yes, there are rules to networking. The first I've already mentioned. I'll repeat it because it bears repeating, then I'll go down the list:

1. Networking is not the same as gossiping. Gossip is personal, intimate and usually hurtful to the person being discussed. Be a professional: Don't gossip. Never speak ill of another author or her work. Your mother was right: If you don't have something nice to say . . .

2. If someone tells you something in confidence, keep it to yourself. It probably shouldn't have been told to you in the first place.

3. Don't pass along unconfirmed rumors. If an author tells you she's heard that the line or house you are targeting your manuscript for is shutting its doors, track this rumor back to its source if possible, or call the house and verify before repeating the news. The publishing business is rife with rumors.

4. You must give in order to receive.

Being an author and a good, effective networker is like climbing a ladder—a very special ladder—one more of experience than success. This one is wider than usual (though not too wide) to allow room for several people on the same rung at once. Instead of going straight up and stopping, this ladder curves over the top, then down the other side and back around again.

Today you may be three "experience" rungs down from the author you just met at a conference. Next year you may be a rung ahead. The year after, she's on top, having gained new experience that you don't yet have. Circular. Evolving. Ever changing. If you take from those above you (those with more experience), everything that is good and right in the universe demands that you hold out a hand to those below (those with less experience) whenever you can.

Not to the point of killing yourself, you understand. You're a writer, after all. You have a career to take care of. Volunteer to help in your local writers group, but don't make it your life's work.

Help when you can, when you're able, when you're willing. But do help. Networking is a tool, and all tools must be kept in good repair in order to perform the function for which they were created. Well-honed networking skills can be a writer's best friend.

So what are you waiting for?

PART 2
General Information

CHAPTER 6

What Are Romance Novels and Who Reads Them?

Rita Clay Estrada

Explaining what constitutes a romance is no easy task. Romance (or women's fiction) reaps the highest retail book sales and yet is probably the most misunderstood fiction genre.

For instance, take any genre—science fiction, suspense, western, time travel—add plot, characterization and the courtship between a male and female, and you have a romance, right? Wrong. That's a romantic story *in* a science fiction, suspense, western or time-travel novel.

A romance is a fictional account of interaction between a male and female. Period. Add science fiction, suspense, western or whatever, and you still have romance. Why? Because the romance is the thread that holds it all together. Everything else, although necessary to move the story along, is secondary to the romance itself.

That means that some of the books we read as romances are really not, and many that are touted as otherwise are really romances in disguise. Why are they so popular? That's simple. Women are problem solvers for their families, and within the pages of these books, problems are stated clearly, solutions are found, different ways of thinking are explored, morals are analyzed, good and evil are emphasized, good deeds are rewarded and vicarious travel is enjoyed. And one more thing: For the time it takes to read one, women are in charge of their own destinies. They have the right to say yes or no to a myriad of choices, change their direction in life, make contact with a recalcitrant child—all this and more. Successful romances share the thoughts, emotions and situations that relate to their readers' own lives.

Inside those pages, women can find themselves, reveal unhealthy pasts, seek answers to their roots, find solutions to anything from troublesome adolescents to unsavory murders, fly to any planet in this universe or others or be the only woman in a gold rush camp—and still just be reading a romance.

In fact, studies prove that romance is a part of life that everyone, i.e., every single and/or lonely female and male, in the world is looking for. Almost everyone wants the intimate companionship of a mate who loves her in return. Numerous songs, poems and self-help books underline how to find the love of your life. Romances highlight those wonderful emotions and memories and present solutions to the myriad problems standing in the way of finding that happiness. Romance novels have uplifting endings that leave the reader feeling good about life, family and loved one.

Is it escapism? You bet. Isn't that the purpose of all fiction? Is it predictable? To an extent. All fiction is. It has been said that people who consistently read have unconsciously located the pattern (read scenes, sequels, complications, plot) in all fiction. They read because they're anticipating that pattern. If they don't find it or if it is too weak, they put the book down and don't finish it. They also don't recommend it to others.

But the story skeleton itself is predictable. Readers know the beginning and ending of each one told. They know mysteries will have a dead body in the beginning and usually a caught killer in the end. They know that science fiction and westerns have the emotional or physical equivalent of a gunfight between good guys and bad guys with good guys finally winning in the end. A romance will have the theme of boy meets girl, boy loses girl, boy gets girl. It will also hold a happy ending or conclusion to that set of stated problems.

As readers and writers, we know A (the beginning) and we can assume we know Z (the end): They are givens. But A and Z are *not* the reason we read. We continue to read for the middle, the B through Y—everything *but* the beginning and end. In other words, we seek our entertainment in books because we want to know all the in-between. We want the why and how. Those are the stuff magic is made of, for which stories are told and books are written.

Even as writers—especially as writers—we're interested in many of the same things. We know how we want our story to begin, and we usually know its ending. What we don't know is how we're going to make the journey reach that end. That's where characterization and plotting come in.

So romance is all around you, and you can't wait to write. What kind? Category? Historical? Science fiction? Period fiction? Regencies? There are many subgenres within the romance genre. I'll touch on a few here.

Category romances are those books for which a publisher generates a set amount of titles (usually two, four or six a month) at the same time. Word count is closely guarded, which dictates the amount of well-rounded characters you can safely structure, the amount of standard-length chapters you will have and how many scenes and sequels you will unfold. Publishers have tip sheets for most categories. Write to the publishing house to request them.

Historical romances are set between 1066 and 1899. They can take place anywhere in the world, but some settings sell better than others. The Southwest and West are currently popular choices. There is no specific word count unless the historical is in a category line. You and your editor will determine it.

Period romances take place from 1900 through the 1940s. They aren't quite historical, but they're certainly not contemporary either.

One major thing these and other subgenres have in common is that they all require thorough research. Facts and figures must be accurate, just as they must be in all fiction. If something is changed or rearranged for the sake of the plot, e.g., a battle, a news story or a trip, it must be stated in a disclaimer.

So you can see that romance as a genre has such a broad scope, it's sometimes hard to define. It can blend into any genre, disguising itself as just plain good fiction.

A few writers have decided they no longer write romances. Instead they write "women's fiction" or "suspense" and so forth. I'm amazed by this. Their audience is made up of mostly romance readers, the largest population of fiction readers in America. However, they are sufficiently worried about hurting the feelings of those readers who believe they *are* romance writers, so they keep their disclaimers very quiet. And they are just as grateful as the rest of us that readers are loyal to good writing—no matter what genre claims it.

So, who's the average romance reader? Harlequin, who does many profiles, has compiled statistics and graciously allowed us to use the fruits of that labor.

Romance readers can be any age, with the average reader being forty years of age. Sixty-three percent are married, 52 percent work outside the home, 22 percent work in the home and 18 percent are retired. Also, the average reader is well educated: 56 percent of current readers attended or graduated college. (43 percent for the average U.S. woman.) You won't be surprised to learn that reading is their primary leisure activity.

If you meet any of those statistics, you're basically writing for yourself. So figure out what makes you turn pages, and you'll have an idea of what the readers want.

Can anyone be a published writer? I have no idea. I do know that it takes more than an understanding of the mechanics of English to sell a book. Books written by new writers are bought every day. Success depends on the individual and how badly he's willing to chase his dream to fruition. This book is just one piece of proof that information is available for you to learn. What's the worst thing that can happen if you've studied and read and still haven't sold? You have learned something new and appreciate the work that goes into it.

Published romance, like all other fiction, has good and bad representations. The good get republished, and the bad have a one-time chance in the sun. Romance Writers of America has the RITA Award for the best published books in the genre, giving them the recognition they deserve. Read them. You'll find the best of the genre at your fingertips. Learn from them. It's one of the best teaching tools in the trade.

Learn all you can about the genre, read all the good books that come your way, talk to others who are willing to discuss what they've learned with you. Remember that no one "owes" you their knowledge; you need to find what appeals to you, discover where your own personal "knowledge holes" are and fill those blind spots by learning on your own. You'll also need a deep-seated respect for the genre and its well-rounded "formula." Keep your thoughts imaginative, your stories fresh, and you're on your way to making your own dream come true.

CHAPTER 7
The Role of the Romance Novel

Deborah Camp

If you are female and have lived sometime in the past sixteen centuries, you've probably been raised on romance stories. From the early origins of Greek and medieval tales through Jane Austen and the Brontë sisters until now with Johanna Lindsey and Nora Roberts, romance stories have entertained us, enlightened us and helped form our feelings about men, marriage and motherhood.

THE TIMELESS APPEAL OF ROMANCE

From the beginning, romance stories were delegated to female readers and not considered true literature, and yet they have prevailed and flourished through the ages. But why? And how?

The why is easy. Romance novels are centered on women and their deepest feelings. The themes might not be ponderous or lofty, but they are heartfelt. In fairy tales such as *Cinderella*, *Snow White* and *Beauty and the Beast*, we learn of heroes and heroines. Some might read these tales with devout frowns and point out that the heroines do nothing but sit and wait for their princes to come, but those critics are not seeing the whole story.

In *Cinderella*, we have a heroine who goes from rags to riches with the help of her belief in love and that wishes can come true. *Snow White* is an awakening story, where a young woman comes into her own and remains steadfastly courageous and honorable when faced with unspeakable evil. Beauty teaches us to make lemonade out of lemons. She is forced into a loveless union with a monster of a man and not only makes the best of it, but sees the hidden, tortured heart of the Beast and learns to love him. She also manages to break a curse while she's at it to free her man from his heinous prison.

From these works, we can begin to see the roots of many romance novel plots: rags to riches, woman in jeopardy, marriage of convenience. These stories appeal to females because they teach lessons of nurturing, of aspiring, of following your heart and of finding success or rewards. Mostly, of course, they speak to us of finding love. As humans, we crave love.

The romance novel has changed as women's roles in society have changed. *Romance* meaning "love story" is a modern use. Until the twentieth century, a romance was a story that included love but that also included many other experiences. Generally, love stories have been disdained throughout history as not being serious or of a true literary nature. Having a woman as the centerpiece of the story and having her prevail and find happiness is hard for many literary critics to stomach. One must throw a monkey wrench into the formula of happily ever after to garner critical success. Infidelity, for instance, as is found in the best-seller *The Bridges of Madison County*, apparently lifted this love story to a different level of general acceptance. Although this novel received its share of critical lampoons, it also earned noteworthy praise.

Those who understand the nature of romance novels are quick to point out that this story is not really a romance in the realm of the current genre, for it deals with infidelity in a kind, even glorified light. Genre romances, those aggressively popular forms of fiction, celebrate one-man/one-woman unions. This thread of morality is woven into love stories from the earliest forms to the present-day Harlequins.

This bright thread of morality is what most critics of romances flail at, not understanding that it is the very heart of romance stories. Unfailing, unflinching fidelity is the perfection women seek in their unions with men. The slow expansion of women's rights in society has not altered this, and it is reflected in romance novels.

Through the earliest forms of the romance to its current transformation, the stories trumpet the individual. The focus is not broad, but narrow, zeroing in on two people who come to mean the world to each other and thus create a world, or a family unit, for each other.

REGENCY—THE ULTIMATE ESCAPE

Romances are often called "escapist fiction," and this is certainly true. Most fiction, by design, is meant to allow the reader to escape into a fictive world. Surely the most escapist of all romance fiction is the Regency, for it whisks the reader to a world of handsome noblemen with vast holdings. While wild and ruthless and blatantly unfaithful, these Regency rogues are tamed by the love of a comely heiress or a penniless but plucky governess. However, the path to true love is never smooth and the Regency hero, like his contemporary counterpart, must battle a variety of foes ranging from unfair society rules to other men who claim their ladies fair.

Authors such as Georgette Heyer, Barbara Cartland, Marion Chesney, Joan Aiken and Jane Aiken Hodge carried the torch of this popular form of romance into the twentieth century from its birth in 1811 when His Royal Highness, Prince of Wales, became Prince Regent after King George III was misdiagnosed and incapacitated. In 1821, King George III died and the prince (of "Georgie-Porgie, puddin' an' pie" fame) became King George IV. Jane Austen is the most famous of these storytellers.

In the early 1800s, Minerva Press began printing the popular Regency romance with such titles as *An Angel's Face and a Devil's Heart* and *Husband Hunters*. These novels often ran into five to ten volumes as the story was fed by its own popularity. Instead of "going back to press" for additional copies, the authors simply penned the next volumes of their voluminous tales.

THE GROWTH OF GOTHIC

From these atmospheric stories of court intrigue and elegant wit, we can see the natural growth of another subgenre referred to as the gothic. Many contemporary romance authors cut their literary teeth on this form of romance because it saw its greatest popularity in the 1960s. These stories of women in jeopardy dominated the romance genre, and their very proliferation is often cited as the reason for their ultimate demise a decade later.

The woman as a victim in these novels battled outside forces to break free of her bonds. It's interesting to note that the covers of gothic novels depicted a young woman fleeing a house, her historically "proper" place in society. These novels were brooding, dark and full of tension. The romance took a back seat to the danger faced by the heroine.

Along with the gothic novel could be found other romantic fare such as Emily Loring's sweet and suspenseful romances and Harlequin's foray into nurse/doctor romances. Powerhouse novelists Mary Stewart, Victoria Holt and Phyllis Whitney moved their stories from the gothic to the romantic suspense and tapped into a faithful readership.

THE ROMANCE BOOM

The romance boom was sounded when a cannonball of a manuscript landed on then Avon editor Nancy Coffey's desk. The manuscript was *The Flame and the Flower* penned by Kathleen E. Woodiwiss, and its publication, like the pathway to love taken by its hero and heroine, was anything but easy. Coffey had to convince her boss, Peter Meyer, the firm's editor in chief at the time, to publish the novel. Their battles on this subject are legendary, with Meyer concerned that the historical romance had been dead since the 1940s when Margaret Mitchell's blockbuster *Gone With the Wind* had reigned supreme and Coffey believing this novel would change all of that. The Woodiwiss book was published in April 1972 and marked the beginning of a publishing gold rush that spanned decades.

Sensuality had come to the romance novel, and writers such as Rosemary Rogers (*Sweet Savage Love*) added their own twist that became known derogatorily as the "bodice ripper." This type of novel was the first to veer toward infidelity, although the heroine did end up with the man she loved above all others. Rape and bondage were found in these stories, and violence became sex's strange bedfellow. The "romantic historical" emerged from these sexy romps and eclipsed them in short order.

Once again women embraced fidelity and eschewed violence directed at heroines by heroes. By the middle of the 1970s, the historical romance boom was in full flower, and the media started to buzz around it like so many curious bees, attracted by the sweet flash of cash. Reports estimated that at least one quarter of all books purchased in America were romances.

Enter Harlequin on the scene, followed quickly by Dell, Berkley and Simon and Schuster. The focus shifted from historical to contemporary tales, and the flamboyant "Queen of Romance," Barbara Cartland, had to make room on the throne for an upstart named Janet Dailey.

Dailey broke through the British stronghold and saw her first Harlequin category romance published to vigorous sales. *No Quarter Asked* opened the door for the American romance.

American readers wanted more than a young, aimless heroine who meets a worldly, driven man and falls in love with him in spite of his rather brusque treatment of her and his unwillingness to share his thoughts or dreams with her. American readers wanted much, much more, and Dailey delivered. Her independent-minded young women matched wits and wiles with her equally independent men and created what editors in the business call "sparks." Dailey had drop-kicked Harlequin into the end zone of opportunity.

Contemporary category romances flourished and gave historicals a run for the money. Janet Dailey became wildly popular, both in the United States and overseas. Her novels were enthusiastically embraced in countries where women were gaining or fighting for equal rights. For instance, her Harlequin novels were big business in Japan, where women struggle to break the bonds of male-dominated tradition.

The 1980s witnessed many changes in romance publishing. The genre became big business and spawned the Romance Writers of America, which held its first conference in 1981 and has since become the largest writers organization in the world.

The romance novel reflected in rapid fashion the changes women were undergoing in society. Stories focused on the struggles of women. Personal independence vs. the desire for a faithful mate was explored, and happy endings were couched by sacrifices made by both the heroine and hero. The increase in the divorce rate in America sprouted stories of single parents and second chances at that one true love.

Author Jayne Ann Krentz found a niche by penning novels in which women and men butt heads and hearts in the workforce. Her books such as *Corporate Affair* and *Power Play* juggle issues of the bedroom and the boardroom.

Gradually, the heroines in romance novels became stronger

willed and upwardly mobile of their own volition. Yes, they wanted a prince, but not just *any* prince. And they wanted something more than just another pretty face. While the covers of the novels failed to change, the novels themselves underwent many alterations from the 1970s to the 1980s.

If Jayne Ann Krentz inserted corporate America into the romance novel, then surely Sandra Brown slipped sizzling sensuality into them. Under the aptly named Ecstasy imprint, Brown penned novels that pitted a sexy hero with an equally sexy heroine. Back in the 1960s and 1970s, the heroines had been confused by the male sex drive and had been unaware of their own sexual prowess, but the 1980s' heroines were enlightened and empowered. Brown created sexually aware heroines in both contemporary and historical venues. Whether it be *Hidden Fires*, a historical romance published by Pocket in 1982, or *Seduction by Design*, a contemporary romance published by Silhouette Desire that same year, Brown's heroines are not only plucky, they are seductive, and her heroes are motorcycle riders in Brooks Brothers suits. Women bought Brown's books by the hundreds of thousands and still do, making her a *New York Times* bestseller author.

While Harlequin could claim Janet Dailey and Dell Ecstasy could claim Jayne Ann Krentz (writing as Jayne Castle), Silhouette trotted out its megastar with a book titled *Irish Thoroughbred*. Nora Roberts took an early lead with this novel and kept gaining ground. Her characters were real and utterly contemporary. Her dialogue was American and full of wit. Laughter became an important ingredient in the romance formula thanks to Nora Roberts. Wiseacre heroines and smirking heroes pushed her books to the top of the romance best-seller lists. Romance readers began talking about "keepers," books they couldn't part with, and Roberts' books became as illusive in used-book stores as Cartland's books were plentiful.

The romance boom was upon the land, and even the harshest critics had to acknowledge the phenomenon. If these books were so bad, why was business so good? Why has the romance novel stayed afloat all these centuries and come to present one half of all mass paperback novels sold in the United States?

They have endured because of the female's insatiable appetite for love in all its guises. Critics expound on the romance novel's lack of literary merit, extremists proclaim the novels as soft pornography, or as somehow evil, dim-witted or illogical, but the women writing for women persevere. These prolific scribes persist because they have stories to tell of their own changing roles in society, their struggles, their frustrations and their triumphs.

Their heroines were and are reflections of themselves and the women around them. Sometimes idealized, yes, but mostly anchored in real experiences, real emotions.

ROMANCE IN THE 1990s

The dawn of the 1990s brought stories of women raising children on their own, of women adopting children without "Mr. Right" beside them, of women of color, of women feeling the crushing weight of trying to have it all, do it all, experience it all. The heroines of the 1990s are still strong, but they are also wise to the perfect pitch a man and woman united can make in this imperfect world. While they will not "settle" for marriage, they are openly seeking a suitable match. The stories mix love with laughter, wit with wisdom and desire with commitment. They also reflect the reining in of sexual freedom. Birth control and, yes, virgin brides and grooms are all discussed in 1990s' romances. Responsibility has become a battle cry, with a deluge of books depicting men as model fathers, accepting the mantle of parenting and partnership.

Historicals, mindful of times when freedom came at a higher price and choices for women were few, if any, continue to be popular. Through these tales, women can see how far they've come, while appreciating the finer traditions of chivalry and chastity. However, these stories have rather modern women in them, appealing to the contemporary reader. For the most part, the historical romance heroines are on the cutting edge: The women are ahead of their times, thus requiring heroes who are more broadminded and tolerant than the average Slade, Blaec or Thorne.

Romance authors now appear with regularity on the national best-seller lists. Authors like Woodiwiss, Brown, Dailey, Lindsey, Roberts and Krentz are joined by other former category romance writers who have leapt onto the best-seller lists, among them Elizabeth Lowell, LaVyrle Spencer, Linda Howard and Karen Robards. Even category romances are breaking into the national best-seller lists after decades of being shut out.

The romance has triumphed because it has changed with its readers to present and ponder the dreams, desires, problems and needs of women. After a long, hard day of bringing home the bacon, cooking it and feeding it to a hungry family, it's nice to know that a happy ending is waiting on the last page of that romance novel.

After all, you don't have to *be* Cinderella to *know* Cinderella. She is found in every girl's dreams, in every woman's heart.

CHAPTER 8

Romance—A Woman's Intricate Journey

Helen Mittermeyer

The great Chinese philosopher Lao Tzu said that the journey of a thousand miles must begin with a single step. It's not exactly that way for a woman on the twisting, turning trip to romance. Perhaps not every woman on the planet is looking for romance, but enough are to validate comments on it. Those who have chosen or will choose the way of romance will be my focus.

Romance in a woman's life is often a travelogue and a search. The innate optimism of those who seek to find romance can lead them to joy or to sorrow. On this intricate journey, there are many threads, such as those tying them to family, tradition and career. Working full- or part-time doesn't lessen the responsibilities at home, especially if a woman is a parent.

To make time for romance a woman has to juggle myriad skills that would make an army platoon blanch. This doesn't sound that romantic. Look again. Today, women often have to be tough, determined and unafraid, all the heroic aspects we apply to romance. These heroines create order out of chaos and don't lose a beat in the rhythm of life. I don't forget this when I write romances.

Not all romantic journeys pay off. Say, for instance, that a woman finds a mate, figuring there will be romance. Children may arrive on the scene. If, for a multitude of reasons, the marriage or liaison doesn't work out, things can change radically. Becoming the primary caretaker, the top wage earner, the designated decision maker can be overwhelming. If the husband goes back to the singles' scene, he could forget the need for boots and braces for the kids. The problems don't go away. Often they escalate. Some romantic trip! In such a scenario it can take years to get even with the world, if ever, and that is an intricate journey.

What about those who find true romance—that loving journey where they are in partnership with others who will share hopes and dreams? I can only say, after writing about women who are successful on the intricate journey, that other women applaud them and want to be like the women they read about and even join them on a journey of their own.

THE ROLE OF THE ROMANCE WRITER

As a romance writer, what's my role in all this? Certainly I don't have a therapist's credentials, nor do I wish to convey that I have professional answers to the problems of modern life. I'm in the entertainment business, so what use am I on this personal journey? Since my readers have commented so many times on how buoyed they can be by reading a romance when their own lives are out of whack, I have to think, in some small way, I'm performing a good deed. When women give me positive responses to my work, saying that it entertains, delights, distracts and relaxes them, I'm more than pleased. When they say I've lifted their spirits, that I've given them impetus to "try again," I'm humbled.

In romance writing, just as in other crafts, art can imitate life. In some ways, a writer can define truths and lies along the romantic highway. She can achieve this by cataloging the bumps in the road and by pointing out the necessity of controlling the ride and not being a passive passenger in dealing with life. In over fifty books, I've managed to show the benefits of a woman controlling her own life. Seeking and finding the right partner along life's highway isn't easy, but I feel it's worth trying. In writing about the journey, I'm able to present various scenarios. Romance novels are entertainment, but no one can say there's nothing to learn from them.

My newest book, *The Veil*, describes an intrepid woman caught in the extreme chauvinism of the fourteenth century. Certainly some of her problems mirror women's problems today. The struggle for identity, for control of one's own destiny, for the ability to have a say in how a life is lived hasn't changed. They are the predicaments of today as they were in the imbroglios of yesterday.

With the written word, the reader can accompany the writer. When we take the reader along on this trip, it's a delightful partnership. When readers enthuse about a book, they join with the writer in a very special way since romance writing is personal and in concert with the reader. When the feedback states that the book was enjoyed, that there was something very applicable to a reader's life, I as a romance writer experience the greatest pleasure.

Author Edith Wharton said there are two ways of spreading light: to be the candle or the mirror that reflects it. To me, being a romance writer means to be both. The candle is my desire and talent for expressing myself in the written word. The light is certainly within me when I put my thoughts, my feelings, my dreams on paper. That I may become, at times, a lantern along the road, a mirror that reflects that light of romance is a joy to me. It's a coup if I can give solace to some, relaxation to most, even righteous anger to a few. After talking to a great many readers over these many years, I sense that's been accomplished.

Learning how women have managed on the road to finding romance, how they've depended on romance novels to entertain and enlighten them has been an eye opener for me. That I can reach out to my gender and give them a hand however small is most rewarding because the often narrow paths that women have to take in order to fulfill their destinies can be arduous. If writing about women who face similar barriers eases their way, alleviates some of the burden, I'm delighted with that.

Some years ago I wrote about the life experiences of my daughter, who, at the time, was a judge advocate general for the Air Force. I was told *Brief Encounter* might never sell. Women wouldn't be interested in a military woman struggling against adversity, unfairness and inequality. Even if I'd agreed with them (and I didn't), I knew I wanted to write the book. I did, and it was a runaway bestseller. The letters I received extolled the intrepidity of the heroine who wouldn't back down, who took on cases others wouldn't handle. Life's kicks and slaps weren't allowed to defeat her because she fought back.

BEYOND THE ROMANCE NOVEL

Is all of life connected to the intricate road to romance? I don't think so. I've met women who want to embark on a trip through a romantic life, but I've also come across a few who'd rather not. Many times they lack imagination and vision. Since fiction writing demands imagination and vision, I have little rapport with the unimaginative. They don't and can't occupy my thoughts in this piece. I can only speak for those who do attempt the journey with effort and determination. It's this type of woman I choose to write about because I deeply espouse the need for courage and good choices on this intricate trip. These yeoman's attempts and the wonderful women who keep trying are what drive me and are mainstays to my writing.

We know there are areas of the world where women have no choices, and little can be done for them without monumental change. I can't affect that. I can aim my work, and I do, toward the women who seek to change and enhance their lives and have a chance at it. I do this by penning such women into my books.

If a woman decides to change her chances, her environment, she can begin an intricate journey of her own. These are the women I write about and believe in because I want to be one. My daughters and daughter-in-law imitate such intrepidity. If there is an underlying meaning in my work, it's that. If one person embarks on the road to romance after reading one of my novels, I'm delighted.

I cannot understand the alleged necessity of disempowering the majority of people on the planet. The attitude that women should be kept at heel is bogus. Yet, women are constantly defending their rights to be in this world. I cannot pretend something I don't believe. I can't give credence to the notion that women are not worthy contenders in every element of life except fatherhood. They must be given room to grow, expand horizons, change directions. I repeat myself when I say the intricate journey is not difficult when good choices are made. Some women find a partner worthy of the appellation "romantic." I was one of those.

Winston Churchill said an appeaser is one who feeds a crocodile—hoping it will eat him last. I'm not an appeaser; I'm a strong stroker for the rights of those who've been denied them for a variety of reasons. I believe caring and crusading belong in women's fiction. I want to continue on the intricate road to romance, entertaining and being a part of that righteous crusade. I invite all with verve and vision along for the ride.

CHAPTER 9
Writing With Passion

Debbie Macomber

One of my favorite fictional characters is the White Queen from Lewis Carroll's novel *Alice in Wonderland*. Every morning before breakfast, the White Queen practiced believing six impossible feats. You're reading this book and, like the White Queen, daring to dream a seemingly impossible dream: a career as a romance writer.

GETTING PUBLISHED: FIRST, SOME BAD NEWS

While the intent of this chapter is to give you an edge over the competition, you first need to hear the bad news.

Author Phyllis Whitney claims there's no good time to sell a book, and the sad truth is, she's right. Selling my first novel was by far the most difficult challenge I've ever faced. I wasn't politely knocking against the door of opportunity either. I pushed and pulled, placing the full force of my grit and determination into the project. I did everything I was supposed to do, dedicating my time, energy and enthusiasm to writing. I was a writer on a publishing quest. Someone was going to read my work, appreciate my genius enough to pay me. Period. But more than my ego was on the line.

By composing stories, I was sharing a part of myself, my dreams, my goals with the rest of the world. In doing so I asked that someone, anyone, please stop, listen and appreciate me.

In the years it took me to sell my first book, I practiced the power of positive thinking. Never had I wanted anything in my life more. Never had I worked harder. Still, it took me four long, grueling years and four completed manuscripts to achieve my goal.

I wish I could tell you that it's gotten easier in the years since, but that would be doing you an injustice. In the last twelve months, dramatic changes have happened within the marketplace. The mid-list is evaporating before our eyes. Superstores are eating away at the independents. Times are hard, and publishers are forced to make adjustments in their publishing programs. Few seem willing to take chances and back new authors as they once did.

In other words, if you're reading this book because you think it'd be fun to be a published author, think again. I'd suggest you take up something less straining, like brain surgery. If you're reading this because there's a fire in your soul, then read on. The best is yet to come.

LOOKING ON THE BRIGHT SIDE

Receiving a publishing contract is difficult, but it isn't an insurmountable task. There's plenty of good news to combat all the negative.

According to a recent survey, 80 percent of all fiction books bought in the United States are purchased by women. Romance makes up 40 to 48 percent of all paperbacks. We as romance readers and writers own a huge chunk of the market.

The world is full of talented writers. Some make it, and some don't. Some simply love the *idea* of being a writer. Unfortunately, no one from a New York publishing house is going to contact you and offer you a seven-figure contract simply because she hears you've taken up writing.

Some time ago I taught a two-day intensive writing workshop. As part of the session, I was asked to critique the attendees' manuscripts. Each writer was instructed to submit fifty pages. Everyone did as instructed with the exception of one woman who forwarded only ten pages. Those few pages revealed a good deal of promise. I was disappointed not to receive more.

Five years later, a friend taught the same two-day workshop, and I discovered that the same woman was back with those same ten pages. In five years she hadn't written a word more. Yet, she'd paid good money to attend this workshop. She's a good example of someone who wanted to be *known* as a writer, of someone waiting for New York to offer her a seven-figure contract.

Over the years, I've judged contests and read countless manuscripts and literally hundreds of books. The talent I've seen in some unpublished manuscripts has literally left me in awe. Without discounting my own talent, I've asked myself how it is that I'm published and these writers aren't. What's made the difference?

Out of all the talented writers in the world, why me? Why did my book sell when there were plenty of other writers out there just as talented, just as committed, just as gifted at storytelling? Some might suggest luck, and I'll be the first to agree that a certain amount of luck played into it. Being at the right place at the right time never hurt anyone. That would account for the first sale, but what about the books that followed? I believe I've discovered the answer.

THE SECRET INGREDIENT FOR SUCCESS

A writer can have all the skill and talent in the world, but unless he conveys his passion and love for the written word, the story, the plot and the characters, his work may never sell. From the beginning, I was passionate about the writing, about every character and story line. Each book is a part of my being, a small piece of my soul. It took time and effort to reach the point where my work was salable, but I didn't give up, didn't "throw in the towel."

Writing is a journey. It's reaching down deep inside of ourselves and extracting the pain, the doubts and the fears that haunt us. It's part of the healing process for us all. Being a writer motivates us to explore life, to pay attention to what's going on around us and what isn't. It's a wake-up call that gives us a reason to be bolder. As writers we find it much easier to forgive ourselves and chalk up our mistakes as occupational hazards: It isn't the devil that made me do it. It was the computer screen!

Like many of my friends, writing wasn't just an option for me. It was something I had to do. In one form or another, I was going to be a writer, and I refused to relinquish that dream.

I believe this passion, this need to express oneself to the world is what makes the difference between those who sell and those who don't. It is the key ingredient that sets one talented writer above another, that causes a publisher to choose one writer over another.

Editors intuitively recognize it. So do agents. Unfortunately, it's only the beginning. A passion for writing, for the story and characters is the starting point. A writer must be passionate for excellence, too.

Several years ago I met a natural storyteller. Ideas bubbled up from her like crude oil gushing out of Prudhoe Bay. I sat back astonished as I listened to her leap from one fabulous idea to the next, rattling them off as easily as reciting the alphabet. She claimed to have written nine books. I was amazed she hadn't sold one until she explained it was her policy to submit her first draft. To her way of thinking, if an editor liked her story idea enough she would ask for revisions.

To the best of my knowledge, she's never sold. I feel she hasn't succeeded because she hasn't given any novel her best effort. She has a passion for stories—plotting and writing—but not for excellence.

How sad. She's eager and talented. She's convinced that some day an editor is going to be impressed enough with her genius to offer her a contract on the sheer energy of her enthusiasm. In many ways, she's like the woman who submitted the same ten pages twice: a wanna-be. Being a wanna-be is fine if you're willing to settle for writing without publication. I couldn't, and if you've continued reading this book, I suspect you won't be able to either.

Often when I speak, I advise my audience participants to imagine holding a book they've created. Imagine people reading *your* words, laughing at all the right places, shedding tears where you shed tears. My mentor and friend, Virginia Myers, told me years ago: "Tears in the writer, tears in the reader." You can't expect your reader to feel the emotion if you don't.

Hold that image of your published book in your mind and refuse to let it go. Don't limit yourself or streamline your dreams. Go for the gusto!

When my editor mailed me my first published book, my heart was flooded with emotion. Here at last was the realization of my dreams, the reward I'd waited so long for. I experienced the identical joy and wonder I did when my newborn daughter was gently placed in my arms. Only this time the labor was much longer! But the compensation was just as satisfying.

Recently I met a Romance Writers of America Golden Heart contest finalist. I congratulated her, recognizing her achievement. Anyone who makes it to the top fifth or sixth place out of hundreds of entries is clearly close to selling. She surprised me by claiming that if she didn't win, she was giving up being a writer. She'd invested two years already and hadn't expected it to take nearly this long.

She didn't win, and I haven't seen her since. I fear this is the fate of many talented writers. They give up; they don't have the heart to continue.

Jayne Ann Krentz wrote for six years before she sold her first novel. At the time, she held a full-time job and wrote from four to seven each morning before leaving for work.

Linda Lael Miller started penning novels when she was in grade school. Her first novel was completed while she was in high school. She filled eighteen notebooks before selling her first novel in her thirties.

I, too, gave it my all, writing every day from eight in the morning until three in the afternoon. After four committed years filled with setbacks and rejections, I reached my goal.

All three of us stuck it out. Ask us if we're glad we did.

CHAPTER 10

Writing With a Partner

Dan and Lynda Trent, aka Danielle Trent

There are as many ways to coauthor as there are people who write together, and what works for one writing partnership may not work at all for another. The reason is that each writer has a unique set of skills and abilities that must be blended with those of another to form a single, cohesive unit. Since the strength of each skill is widely variable, the ways the skills are combined are different for every writing partnership. The success of the team, therefore, is dependent upon the existence of all the necessary skills within the unit, the strength of those abilities, the manner in which they are blended and a high level of cooperation.

WHY COAUTHOR?

The first question to answer is "Why do you want to do this in the first place?" Most who have never tried coauthoring believe it would be easier to write with someone than to write alone. After all, as a team you always have someone to commiserate with over rejections, writer's block and so forth. However, it doesn't always work that way. Your partner may commiserate with you over your inability to produce on occasion. But if it happens too often, affecting the ability of the team to make a living or meet its deadlines, you may find your easygoing, mild-mannered partner going ballistic.

There are teams who write together successfully while living many miles apart, but they are rare birds seldom seen. And their telephone bills probably rival the national debt. It's much easier to write together if you can sit in the same room occasionally and talk out plots, characterizations, problems with work and the like. However, it is difficult, if not impossible, to do the actual writing together. Writing, like skydiving, is done pretty much alone. There may be others jumping out of the plane with you, but you're better off pulling your own rip cord.

For us to prescribe the best way for you to coauthor with another writer would be as dangerous as a brain surgeon operating on himself. However, there may be some value in an explanation of how we work together, since that question is often put to us, so long as you bear in mind that it is only one example.

PICKING A PARTNER

Although it may seem logical that your best friend, who is also interested in writing, would make the ideal coauthor, it doesn't always work out. Lynda once tried writing a novel with her best friend. Not only had they been best friends for ten or more years, they had been roommates in college and were godparents to each other's children. In a short time, it became obvious that either the book had to go or the friendship. They kept the friendship. There is a different give-and-take in friendship than there is in a business partnership. The priorities are different.

The same probably goes double for writing with a family member. If you discover along the way that your mother can't write well enough to be published, how do you tell her? If your sister has great plot ideas but you don't learn they aren't commercial until they don't sell, can you end your attempt at coauthoring without turning your family reunions into a battlefield?

A lot of people want to write with their spouses. Not only would this keep all the money earned in the same bank account, but there's a rumor that this will bring a couple closer together. Sometimes that actually happens. We enjoy being coauthors, but our marriage was woven in with our writing from the start. Since there has never been a time when we didn't write together, it's more likely our marriage might become strained if we were to stop. That's not to say we don't have some lively discussions about writing from time to time.

Consider who will do what part of the work. If you have to put *your* words on paper or die, and you are good at doing it quickly, you wouldn't want to team up with someone who feels the exact same way. A better choice would be someone who is not as adept at getting the words on paper but who has a good handle on the mechanics, sentence structure, grammar and punctuation, and a knack for subtle reorganization of thoughts and ideas that gives a work the timing and pacing necessary to maintain the reader's interest. This leaves you free to write the rough draft, and your partner can do the rewrites, corrections and revisions.

LEGAL CONSIDERATIONS

Can't coauthoring be as easy as just deciding to work together with another writer? Sure it can. But we all know it isn't prudent to drive your automobile without insurance; accidents can happen even to the most careful of drivers. In our opinion, it isn't wise to enter into a coauthoring relationship without some protection as well. Our recommendation is that a legal contract should be drawn up between coauthors, even if you're the best friends in the world. Put everything in writing.

One provision in the contract should address how things will be handled if one of you decides to end the partnership. This is something that should be decided before the idea enters either of your heads. Working together is difficult and is going to add stresses to the relationship that neither of you may have considered. Spouses get transferred, babies are born, divorces happen, people die. There are many things that can cause a perfectly good partnership to dissolve.

Not the least of the considerations that must be addressed is which of you will be allowed to continue using the pseudonym. It is not uncommon for coauthors to decide ahead of time that neither will be able to use the pseudonym outside of the partnership. Sometimes stipulations in a publisher's contract will control that outcome. All endings aren't peaceful, no matter how close the two of you are at the beginning.

Another factor to consider is whether one or both of you will get the proceeds from any manuscript in progress at the time the partnership breaks up. Which of you gets to finish the uncompleted manuscript? If neither is willing to finish the work, the publisher may want it's advance money back, and how much will each of you owe the publisher? Decisions such as this must be made ahead of time, or the cost of litigation to resolve them may be devastating to both authors.

DEVELOPING A SYNOPSIS

Early on in the process a story line must be determined. Through a free exchange of thoughts and ideas, we brainstorm numerous scenarios and character types until we come across one idea that is compelling to both of us. Together we develop a general idea of the beginning, middle and end of the story. Then Dan turns those thoughts into the plot outline, or synopsis. Next, Lynda, who is stronger on character development, makes whatever plot adjustments she feels are necessary to ensure compatibility between characters and plot, then turns the synopsis back to Dan.

This refinement process continues through as many iterations as necessary until both agree the synopsis is ready to be presented to a publisher. (For the most part, our books are sold from the synopsis alone. Although some publishers will buy a first book from a synopsis and the first few chapters of manuscript, we strongly advise you to complete the entire manuscript before submitting it in order to reduce stress that can inhibit creativity.) In our case, we send the synopsis to our agent, who submits it to an editor at the publishing company.

THE NEGOTIATION PROCESS

It is possible to agent your own work, though it's more difficult, and you'll have to decide which one of you will handle those submittals. If you elect to seek representation by a literary agent, you and your partner may be faced with yet another compromise if each of you has a different agent in mind. (We never said this was going to be easy.)

Agented or not, if the editor wants to acquire the book (technically, the work is licensed), you and your writing partner will have to agree on whether to accept the terms offered or counter-offer in an attempt to get better terms. If you and your partner disagree on any of the numerous terms being offered, the licensing will not go through, and your writing partnership will likely be on rocky ground. On the other hand, if this process of negotiation is successful and you, your coauthor and the publisher agree on every aspect of the deal, including the pseudonym to be used, all parties must sign the contract drawn up by the publisher.

You must never argue with your writing partner in the presence of your editor or prospective editor. One of you should be chosen to conduct negotiations, and a united front should be presented. Not only must your manuscript be written with one "voice," but business dealings must also be done with one voice, even when both of you are talking with your editor.

WRITING THE MANUSCRIPT

Whether it is at this point, as it is in our case, or whether it is done before submittal to a publisher, the manuscript must be written. You may decide on one of you to write the entire first draft (for us it is Lynda because she is much faster). Or you may choose to write alternate chapters, or even particular scenes. Do it however it works best for you. We know coauthors who have divided the writing in all of these ways. The important thing is to get it on paper and do it in a way that it has only one voice. Sentence structure, use of idioms and metaphors, even vocabulary must be consistent throughout. The manuscript must appear to have been written by one person, and that isn't always easy to accomplish.

In our division of labor, Dan does the rewriting, revision, proofreading and polishing of the work. But before the manuscript is sent to the editor, Lynda goes over it at least once more. You may choose to share these tasks. However it is done, objectivity at this point is absolutely necessary. Tact and effective communication are essential as well.

THE EDITING PROCESS

Once the manuscript is accepted by your editor (sometimes after she has recommended additional revisions), typically you will see it twice more before it is printed and bound. The first will be after editing, and the second will be in galley (typeset) form. One or both of you should read the edited manuscript to be sure you agree with all the changes and to correct any errors that may have gone undetected. Minor changes may be permitted at this time, but don't think of this as an opportunity to do the revisions you didn't take time to do before submitting it. Changes to the galley version should be limited to the correction of typographical errors only. One or both of you should read the galley.

A vitally important thing to remember is that you aren't your work. To write is to be criticized. If it's not a coauthor wanting something changed, it's an agent or an editor. It always happens. So it's extremely important to realize from the beginning that when someone finds fault with your work, he is not attacking you as a person. This is probably the single most important lesson for coauthors. "I'm not my book" should be tattooed in a prominent place on each of your bodies, or at least made into samplers to hang on the walls of your offices.

COMMUNICATING WITH YOUR PARTNER

Communication is extremely important between coauthors. If a problem arises, deal with it while it is small. If you assume it will clear itself up or become less important in the future, you may have an unpleasant surprise coming.

This communication should involve not only the way you work together and how you feel about it, but it should include your short- and long-range goals as well. Do you intend to write only one book? Do you see yourselves turning out books well into the twenty-first century?

Stay in communication every step of the way. This is not to say you should drive your coauthor nuts with constant phone calls. But if you run into problems with the plot or characterization, or if the part you agreed to do is more difficult than you can accomplish, talk it over. Writing the rough draft may sound simpler than revisions before you try it. Writing the outline may sound like a piece of cake until you're halfway through the story line and discover you already have enough material for a thousand-page novel and you were shooting for three hundred fifty.

Never lie to your partner. Lies come home to roost at the least opportune time. Some of the most popular lies:

"Of course I've finished the rough draft."

"I mailed the manuscript to the editor yesterday."

"Maybe you never heard of the Isle of Magoombo and the native dance of the flying pig, but I found research to back up everything I wrote."

And the old favorite, "I'll finish it on time if I have to spend all weekend working on it."

Lying to your partner is not professional. After all, this is not something you are doing just for fun; it is a business arrangement and should be handled in a businesslike manner in all respects.

DIVIDING THE MONEY

Another consideration is the money you'll make. Some writers have other sources of income and can afford to wait a long time, if necessary, for a book to sell. Others have a more immediate need and less tolerance for delays. The same goes for the amount of money you believe your product to be worth. In order to get a first novel published, you may be willing to accept whatever royalty rate and advance against royalties the publisher initially offers for fear your partnership will be labeled as uncooperative. In most cases, reasonable negotiation with a publisher is no cause for prejudice. However, if your coauthor feels the work is far more valuable than what is being offered and insists that his demand be met, the sale may be lost and subsequent attempts to sell to that publisher may be adversely affected.

How the money from a coauthored work is divided is also important. We have always agreed that our contributions to our joint writing projects are equal and most often have received separate but equal checks from our publishers. If you and your partner have decided on some other ratio, say sixty-forty, or perhaps the two of you have incorporated or have formed some sort of legal partnership, it is imperative that you notify your publisher of these things prior to the contract being drawn up.

SOME PRACTICAL CONSIDERATIONS

Another decision you'll have to face is what name to write under. You could use a combination of your names or the names of your respective children or pick one out of thin air. It's important to find one you both like because you may be signing it in fan's books for many years to come.

Assuming your book has sold and autographing sessions have been set up, you have to decide if one or both of you will appear as the author. We always autograph together and this is what we recommend, if it's not impossible for you both to be there. Be aware, though, that a surprising number of people have trouble grasping the notion of two (or more) people writing a book. They seem to prefer believing that one of you really wrote it and the other is just coasting along with you. If, on the other hand, only one of you signs the books, the one always left at home may become resentful. Your fans may also become resentful if they learn in the future that two of you wrote their favorite book but only one of you was presented as the author. Only you and your partner can decide which is best.

Another downside to being coauthors is that you will be charged double when you go to conferences or have to travel somewhere. This is more of a problem to spouses or family members who write together since friends usually assume they will travel and pay separately anyway. Although you have only one literary voice, you have two bodies. Work this to your advantage by going separate ways once you've reached the conference and covering twice the territory.

Although there are difficulties and complexities to coauthoring, there are also advantages, such as having the pleasure of working with someone who is every bit as interested in your career as you are. Also, you can bounce ideas off a coauthor when your brain refuses to sequence properly and you have no notion whether your idea makes any sense. It also stimulates creativity to swap ideas. With a coauthor, you have someone who likely shares your feelings toward your agent/editor, whether positive or negative, as strongly as you do. Best of all, you have someone to pull you back down to earth when you start floating into the ethers or zooming off at an odd tangent. The perfect coauthor won't let you tell the agent/editor what you really think about her, or let you sell everything you own so you can move to a deserted island and live on coconuts while you try to compose the greatest novel ever written.

Another big advantage is that you can work on more than one project at a time. We always have at least two novels in progress. While Lynda is writing a rough draft for one, Dan is writing the outline for the next book or polishing the draft Lynda has just finished. Quite often, an edited manuscript or galley arrives in our mailbox and must be reviewed within fourteen days, thus giving us three projects in work at one time.

By the way, a sense of humor is important in team writing. This is possibly the closest relationship you will ever have with another human being and, thus, the most stressful. There will be times when you'd better be able to laugh about it or else.

Coauthoring can be the best and the worst of all relationships.

Usually it hovers somewhere in the middle. If the team stays together, a marriage of sorts happens, and you grow alike in subtle ways. A good team can emphasize the positive aspects and minimize the negative ones. But like a marriage, the team will need care and tending all along the way to ensure its survival. If it endures, it may be the most satisfying relationship you'll ever know.

CHAPTER 11

How Selling a Book Changes Your Life

Christina Dodd

One day the phone will ring. You'll pick it up and an angel on the other end will announce, "You are now a published author."

Please note: This momentous transformation occurs in the space of one second. One second you're unpublished and know nothing. Next you get "the phone call," you're published and the knowledge of the universe suddenly resides in your bosom.

OK, so it didn't happen to me that way, but I know it happened to everybody else.

Everybody else had properly prepared for this moment. They had familiarized themselves with every aspect of the publishing industry. They knew the difference between a copyedit and a line edit. They had sucked up to the right authors so they could ask for a publicity quote. They understood the legalities of a contract. Most amazing, they weren't insulted when booksellers asked if they were getting a "dump."

Me, I could have used a special conference. It would be called BAFFLED, I think—*Beginning Author Frankly Flummoxed by Literary Etiquette and Deadlines.*

The first session would have been Phone Conduct With Your Editor, or Call Early, Call Often, the Long-Distance Companies Need the Cash.

Editors are people, too. My editor happened to be a female

people. The first time she called me to tell me how enthusiastic she was about my book, I could hardly hold the phone because my palms were so sweaty. I was mouth-breathing, and my voice shook. This won't happen to you, of course (see the second paragraph: knowledge of the universe), but my editor was very polite to me, although to this day I imagine she got off the phone and giggled uncontrollably.

After that, I gained a little confidence. At some point it dawned on me she was not the angel conferring all the knowledge of the universe upon me. Or if she was, she had been sadly remiss because I hadn't gotten any, let alone *all*.

As it was, I made dreadful mistakes, the kind of mistakes that are publishing legend, and all because I didn't call for information unless absolutely, positively necessary. I needed that phone seminar, taught by the ghost of my first grade teacher. She'd have slapped my hand with a ruler and said, "If you have a query, call your editor. She is your liaison to your publishing company. She knows you're a new author, and she's perfectly willing to answer questions, regardless of how trivial or stupid. Better to bother her now than to make a costly blunder later."

An addendum to this session would have been Discussing Sex With Ease and Maturity.

The first time I wrote a love scene, I kept glancing over my shoulder. I was embarrassed, I didn't want to get caught and I wasn't sure I was doing it right!

Eventually, I grew to enjoy writing love scenes, but I never imagined I would have to dissect a love scene word by word with my editor. For me, such frankly intimate discussions have been limited to my husband, and he's a *man*.

The teacher of this seminar would *not* be the ghost of my first grade teacher. No, no, she'd be a diminutive sexual therapist with a foreign accent who would say, "Sex is a perfectly natural function, and your job is writing about it well. Your editor's job is to make sure it furthers the plot, heightens the tension and is satisfying to the reader. So get over it—and it's time to call long distance and review your heroine's deflowering."

And I would—while waiting for the next seminar, What to Do With All the Money, or Don't Quit the Day Job.

At the time I was published, I'd been writing for years with the secret conviction that I was a fraud. I thought the writing police were going to break down my door, read my first attempt at a novel and take me away in chains. And considering my first attempt, they probably should have.

Instead, I put thousands of words and three novels behind me before I got that magic phone call. I was told I would be paid for writing, an activity I usually received rejection for. It was a heady affair, and I scarcely retained enough self-control not to beg to be allowed to do it for free. Worse, I was pleased with the piddling amount the publishing company wanted to pay me.

Hell, I was *grateful*.

So I really, really needed a seminar taught by the ghost of Howard Hughes. He'd say, "This is a business. The publishing company is not publishing you as a favor or because it feels sorry about all those previous rejections. It's publishing you because people think they can sell your books. In other words, you are earning the money they send you."

He would also say, "You are now self-employed. Does the term *quarterly IRS payments* mean anything to you? How about *SEP-IRA*? It doesn't? Then get a good investment counselor."

I would have listened to Howard Hughes.

I really needed a seminar called Your First Deadline, or In Comparison, Running a Marathon Is Easy and Fun.

A deadline. It even sounds ominous. If you don't make it, are you dead?

Yes.

I sold my first book as a complete manuscript. Then the publishing company waved money in my face, and I said I could write another book for them. They asked how long it would take me. I said six months.

Heck, what did I know? I hadn't ever had a deadline before. I'd set my own deadlines, but if the kids got sick or work from that other life interfered, I could forget about writing. Now, suddenly, I *had* to finish the book in the time allotted, and I panicked. I cut back on everything that didn't pertain to writing and barely finished the book on time. I had discovered an author's first rule of deadline: The amount of time needed to finish a book will automatically expand two weeks past the time you have.

Who would teach this seminar? Without a doubt, Phineas Fogg. He'd say, "Anything can be done properly with a schedule. Count the number of days you have to write, and count realistically. Take out time for holidays, sick days and play days. Divide the final number into the number of pages you'll have in the book, and you'll know how many pages you have to write a day. Then do it. Do it to the exclusion of all else. Practice saying no to everyone who wants a piece of your time. School, church, organizations can all get along without you. Don't volunteer. Do more for less, and get your book in on time."

Looking back, I had some rather bizarre expectation of the role I would play in my own debut. Not that I consciously thought about it. I just assumed someone at my publishing company would interview me and make a bio that listed my accomplishments, my charms and qualifications. I thought a makeup artist would show up at my house and perform the next best thing to plastic surgery, followed by a photographer who would pose me artfully and make me look as thin as a model.

I didn't realize that I had to assemble my own press release. I never imagined I would have to write about myself in glowing terms and spend my advance on a professional photographer. It all seemed so narcissistic, so I would have gratefully attended a seminar called Promote Yourself or Die as given by Ivana Trump.

"You have just become a celebrity. Probably not a national celebrity, but certainly a local celebrity, and the public has a perception of romance writers that will not die. All romance writers are twenty years old, five feet, eight inches tall, weigh 120 pounds and have long, flowing locks of raven/auburn/sunshine hair. If you don't meet that criteria, they'll be disappointed, so have your portrait done by a professional photographer.

"Look around at the press releases you see in your local newspaper, and use them as a model for yours. This isn't bragging, it is simply listing your accomplishments and presenting yourself in the best light possible.

"Dress professionally whenever you make a public appearance, whether at an autographing or at an interview. Romance suffers from a difficult media image, so maintain your dignity and, most important, your sense of humor."

Everything Ivana addressed is speaking about the private person. For me, the most essential seminar would have been Public Speaking for Authors, or I'm Not Really Nervous, the Tectonic Plates Are Shifting.

I hadn't been published a week when my local writers group

called and asked if I would speak to its monthly meeting, sort of as an inspiration.

I didn't do it. I mean, were they *crazy*? I had been a basket case in Speech 101, and what had I been doing in the years since then? Sitting in front of a computer in baggy sweats, alone, making up dialogue for characters who lived only in my head. I didn't yet understand how people's perceptions of me had changed. According to them, the knowledge of the universe not only conferred upon me authority on all subjects, but came with a little side benefit: the gift of keeping people enthralled with my wit and eloquence.

No one understood or cared that I had ducked when those gifts were flung at me.

Little did I know it, but the writers group was the first flake of an avalanche. Everyone asked me to speak. A local sorority. The Librarian's Association. A church group. I kept saying I couldn't, and they kept laughing gaily and telling me not to be so modest.

Finally, they wore me down. It was sneaky how they did it. One lady asked me to speak to her country club fully eight months before the actual speaking date, and I said yes. A lot of things can happen in eight months. We could move. I could develop a debilitating disease. The writing police could finally catch up with me.

None of those things happened, and I was stuck.

For weeks before, I had nightmares about my contact lenses fogging, of tripping when I walked to the podium, of forgetting my speech. I wrote down every word I wished to say, becoming a public reader rather than a public speaker. And I did, well, OK.

As the result of that speech, I was asked to speak to another group because when it comes to writing, any kind of author, but especially a published author, is the expert.

Definitely this seminar should be taught by Henry Higgins. To this class filled with ineloquent writers, he would say, "Public speaking terrifies more people than any other phobia, and there's only one way to get over it: You have to do it. Don't wait until you're published to start, but start small. Introduce other speakers. Do miniseminars. Speak about what you know well, and say yes to everyone who asks you. Do it until you've had so many good speaking experiences your terror diminishes to a reasonable level. And don't whine."

As an addendum to this seminar, how about one called Private Speaking, or Just Because They Promised It Would Be Kept Confidential Doesn't Mean They Won't Tell a Few Hundred of Their Friends.

There exists a perception that when you are published, you become "someone." This startled me because I had never perceived myself as "no one." All I know is that after that "You are published" phone call, my conversation carried a weight it had never carried before.

I, of course, found out the hard way. When I was first published, I saw no reason not to inform everyone of my advance and my print run. I didn't understand why my editor was annoyed by my candor, nor did I understand how she'd found out that I'd been so frank.

I also spoke freely of not only my troubles, but my triumphs. It startled me to realize that some other writers, both published and unpublished, truly relished my troubles. They were, I suspect, the same writers who belittled my triumphs and loudly suggested that my ego didn't bear examining. And perhaps they were right.

Anyway, this seminar needs to be taught by Eliza Doolittle—in her best English and with her best street smarts. "You're going to change from an awed kid with smudges on your face to an accomplished person disciplined by both achievement and sorrow. Make the transition as easy on yourself as possible. Remember that publishing is a small, closed business and what is said in Houston this morning is repeated at lunch in New York. If you're in doubt, don't say it.

"No one really needs to know about your contracts and your money, and you can spread the word about your awards and your best-seller lists via a newsletter editor or well-placed press releases.

"Word of your failures will spread by itself.

"Never, ever compare your career to someone else's. There's always someone who is doing better. There's always someone who is doing worse. You'll embarrass the one who is doing better and belittle the one who is doing worse, so again, if you're in doubt, don't say it."

Finally, there should be a seminar entitled You Can't Please Them All, or What They Think of You Is None of Your Business.

Who's going to teach this seminar? Honey, I am.

I have progressed through my publishing life slowly and painfully, learning the lessons all the other authors instinctively understood on the moment of their publication. I learned to speak to my editor about both the publishing industry and sex. I learned that I earned my money fairly and how to handle it. I learned about self-promotion and public speaking and private speaking. I became the perfect author, and I did it all the hard way—without the angel's gift of universal knowledge.

Then one day while being the perfect author, I had an imperfect response. Somebody didn't like the perfect author. How could this be?

And I had an epiphany.

It doesn't matter whether you're modest or boastful, it doesn't matter if you're polite or rude, it doesn't matter if you work for the good of others or work only for yourself. You'll win a contest that someone else lost. You'll be on a best-seller list someone else missed. You'll make a deadline someone else fumbled. You'll say something that someone will misinterpret.

So, be aware, you can't please all of the people all of the time.

Writing can consume your life, but stay in touch with the friends who knew you before you were published. They retain the remarkable view that you're just a normal person who worked hard and got a phone call that gave you employment. Old friends like you for yourself, not for your position or what they can get out of you.

Hug your family a lot. They'll make sacrifices for your career, but don't let them be a sacrifice to your career.

Be polite and friendly to other authors, but be aware some of them think that if they bring you down, they'll step into your place.

Choose your writing friends wisely, and confide your publishing woes and triumphs only in them.

Most of all, don't take the business end of things too seriously.

Someone did a survey and asked women what their dream job was, and romance writing came in second (goddess came in first). I imagine that the women who answered this survey think that every book romance writers write is published, that romance writers make so much money we have maids to care for our palatial homes and so much time left over from writing that we attend one Hollywood party after another.

They want the dream; they don't want the reality. And the reality is that this career, like any other, takes talent, perseverance and training. By the time you receive that angel phone call, you know that. You also know that writing is what you want to do.

I didn't get the knowledge of the universe when I got that phone call, but I don't need it to know that I'll always be a writer. Maybe someday I'll be Barbara Cartland, in my nineties and still a bestseller. Maybe I'll be a has-been, chaining my grandchildren to my knobby knees and making them look at scrapbooks filled with my long-vanished publishing triumphs. But I'll still be spinning stories. Because you won't believe how many *New York Times* lists my grandchildren will think I was on.

Even though no angel dumped it on me, I did instinctively know at least a small portion of the knowledge of the universe. I confer it on you. It is this:

The actual act of writing is the most awful job in the world, except when it's the most wonderful, and for those of us who exist in the world of publishing, it's our reward. Writing is our reward for talking to editors, for promoting ourselves, for being discreet, and for making our deadlines. Always remember why you got into this business.

It's not for the respect.

It's not because you enjoy having your ego shredded by editors and readers.

It sure ain't for the money.

You got into writing because you like to tell stories.

You got into romance because there are millions of people who believe the love between a man and a woman is worth exalting.

You got into romance writing because romance reading makes millions of people happy—and because you and you alone become their angel, conferring upon them the gift of a dream.

PART 3
The Craft

CHAPTER 12

Researching Historical Facts

Roberta Gellis

The purpose of researching a historical novel is to provide a realistic and believable background in which characters can live. Some writers dread research, and others adore it, but no writer can afford to allow personal response to decide the depth and detail of the research to be done. That judgment must be made on the basis of how much history is going to be useful to the plot.

Those writing costume drama, the predominant type of historical romance today, should remember that they need touch only lightly on the historical background. The plot of a costume drama is character driven and should not be cluttered up with historical facts of too much description. The historical novel, with its history-driven plot, needs much more detailed research; in such books, the background is often as important as the characters, and much of the life of the novel comes from the accurate details about historical events, food and dress, and manners and mores.

In the past, there were only two sources for historical facts: printed matter, such as newspapers, magazines, books, letters and memoirs, and experts who had already consulted the printed matter or lived through the events the writer wished to depict. Now another source exists: the information superhighway, through which anyone who has the equipment and know-how can reach both experts and printed matter and bring them directly to her own computer screen.

Because some writers do not have the equipment to reach the Internet, I will deal with library resources first.

NAVIGATING THE LIBRARY

While the library may seem like an old, familiar friend, I find certain books a substantial help in using this almost too-abundant source. *The New Library Key* gives detailed information about the catalogs and classifications systems used in the library. *The Modern Researcher* is less detailed but explains card catalogs and computerized catalog systems and offers advice on using them. A truly wonderful assistant, and an affordable one that you can have in your own home, is *Reference Sources: A Brief Guide*, by Eleanor A. Swidan. The book is divided into two parts: Part one lists reference books of general scope, such as encyclopedias, dictionaries and bibliographies. Part two lists reference books according to special subjects, like the humanities and the social and physical sciences.

If you are working on a costume drama, you might wish to confine your historical research to the material in a good encyclopedia and specialized dictionary. For biographical, geographical and historical articles about Europe, the ninth or eleventh editions of the *Britannica* are preferable to more recent editions, which place greater emphasis on scientific and technological subjects and on very recent history.

Since there is a limit to the length of any encyclopedia, something must go. In the *Britannica*, biographical articles about persons before the nineteenth century, and colored plates of historical uniforms have been deleted or condensed. A similar problem exists in the *Americana*, with its emphasis on science and technology. But it does have some excellent biographical articles (many more on American personages than the *Britannica*) and a particularly good section on costume.

For more extensive and varied biographies, however, the *Dictionary of National Biography* (commonly called the *DNB*) for British researchers and the *Dictionary of American Biography* (commonly called the *DAB*) for American researchers are best, and most libraries have them either in print or on microfilm. Important people in these works may have articles as long as five to ten pages of small print in double-column text. The *DNB* and *DAB* are particularly useful when one wishes to include as characters less exalted historical personages than kings and presidents; biographies are offered of those who are not important enough to be mentioned in an encyclopedia. Another valuable asset of the *DNB* and *DAB* are their indexes. From these, which provide the dates during which the persons listed lived, one can garner a complete cast of real characters to support the fictional hero and heroine.

USING INTERLOAN AND MAIL ORDER

For those who would like more information than can be provided by the kind of sources mentioned above, wider use of the library must be made. If your library has a computerized catalog, you will notice that many of the books mentioned are not on the shelves. Your librarian may be able to suggest a substitute or even a more adequate source of information or may be able to obtain the book through interloan. Having mentioned interloan, let me make a few points about general use of a library system.

First, be sure to ask whether your library is part of an interloan system. Often the librarian will not voluntarily mention the system since it makes extra work to obtain books through it. Although the interloan librarian in my own small local library always looks as if she wants to get under the desk when I approach, rare and difficult-to-produce books have been found for me and obtained from university libraries all over the country.

Second, if you find no mention at all of the subject in which you are interested in the card catalog or electronic catalog or the computer brings up only books that do not pertain to your subject area, this may mean you are looking under the wrong word or words. For example, in the computer system used by my local library, "library, use of" does not bring up references like *The New Library Key*, but it does bring up studies on library usage. If you run into a similar problem, consult the librarian for a hint about what wording to use.

Third, if you are not near a library, research books may be obtained from mail-order booksellers, such as Barnes & Noble (126 Fifth Avenue, New York, New York 10011), Dover Publications, Inc. (31 East Second Street, Mineola, New York 11501) and the Scholar's Bookshelf (51 Everett Drive, Princeton Junction, New Jersey 08550), or from many university presses. Any of the three discount houses and any university press will be glad to send you a catalog if you write and request one. This is, of course, a more expensive proposition than free use of a library, but many of the books offered by the discount houses (and even some by the university presses) are not costly, and delightful adjuncts can be found in the catalogs, like the coloring books and costume paper dolls sold by Dover Publications. These are quite accurate from the eighteenth century on as the clothes are reproductions of those in the fashion magazines of the period. Barnes & Noble offers a fascinating set called the See Inside Series, which exposes sectionally a castle, an ancient Greek town, a Roman town, an ancient Chinese town, an Egyptian town and a galleon.

RESEARCH TIPS

Once you know how to use the library, the information available may seem overwhelming. Where and how does one start? Let me suggest the children's library. No, I am not insulting you. Although I have spent nearly forty years researching one or another historical period and geographical place, I still go back to the children's library to start anything new.

Most likely you already know the period and place in which you intend to set your novel, but if you do not or are looking for a new idea, try a children's book on world history. Such a book takes only a few hours to read and will present events in the most dramatic way possible. And children's books are especially good at describing how people lived. One of the best books I have ever found on castles was a library discard from the children's section (*Castles*, by R. Allen Brown).

A great help in research, once period and place are decided, is to choose a limited time period in which one or two climactic events, such as a great battle with far-reaching results or statehood for a territory, have taken place. Such a choice gives adequate scope for individual adventures for the heroine or hero, limits the amount of historical explanation one must give the reader and greatly simplifies the research. The state or territory will certainly have a name, and most battles do, too; thus, you are immediately provided with a specific word to look up in the electronic subject index of your library, in encyclopedias and in the indexes of historical texts and biographies to pinpoint which books will be useful for your purposes.

In addition, the people involved in the adoption of statehood or the battle—not only those who fought for it or in it but those whose policies caused or directed it—will be named. Reading about the individuals involved in any historical event can not only illuminate situations surrounding that event, but also may present it from a more personal point of view. In fact, a good scholarly biography (from the adult section of the library this time) will provide a multitude of types of information and read like a novel, too. Not only will you get the history of the period, but you will find discussions on the manners and mores of the time and descriptions of clothing, the places in which the people lived, the meals they ate, the methods by which they traveled. Often there will be quotations of letters or diaries—the very best way to learn how the people of your period thought and expressed themselves. Perhaps expense accounts will be printed from which one can learn what people of your period spent for food, lodging, clothing and furniture and how much they gave to charity.

Secondary sources (that is, books about history written in modern times) provide summaries of historical facts presented in a clear and straightforward format. Such books can be found by looking under the country and period, for example, "British history" and the date, in the library catalog (card or electronic) or in *Books in Print* or in a bibliography, such as those listed in "Research Bibliography." Secondary sources themselves are also likely to contain bibliographies containing even more references that may be accessed using a computerized search system.

It will rarely be necessary for the writer of historical romance to consult primary sources—those that were actually written in the period you are studying. However, should you need to consult them, they are not hard to find. Biographies, as I mentioned, have bibliographies, and many of the works listed will be primary sources, like diaries and collections of letters.

Let me warn you, however, that a primary source is not necessarily more reliable than a secondary source. For example, before modern times, the idea that a historian should be objective would have been considered laughable. For early historians, your friends and allies were good, your enemies were evil, and that was that. As you know, this attitude has not been wholly extirpated from the modern mind; however, the reputable modern historian is *supposed* to struggle for an impersonal view that presents all aspects of an event.

The problem of making your historical novel come alive can be solved with the help of the many books available describing the ways of life in all times and places. Again try the YA (young adult) or children's section of the library first. A book for children often has clearer, more dramatic illustrations and more interesting details than books for adults. You will find many titles starting with *Life in*, or *Everyday Life in*, such as *Life in a Medieval City*, by Joseph and Frances Gies, or *Everyday Life in Medieval Times*, by Marjorie Rowling.

There are also many books on costume; I have found those by Yarwood, such as *European Costume*, clear and simple. Most of the discount mail-order booksellers mentioned earlier will have several costume books available at reasonable prices.

Even more books have been published about food. Many of these are utterly delightful because they include commentary or quotes from the period in which the recipes were recorded. *Pepys at Table* with recipes and extracts from Pepys's famous diary gives not only dishes and their preparation but songs and illustrations from the seventeenth century. *To the King's Taste*, also illustrated and provided with careful explanations, does a similar job for the time of Richard II. And Dover has published a facsimile edition of *American Cookery 1796*, by Amelia Simmons.

Few other details of life in the past remain unexplored. Books on medicine, on gardens, on architecture and on furniture are all readily available.

Clothes change, cities change, methods of travel change, but people's emotions, although their motives and the causes that bring forth these emotions differ, change very little. Proof of that can often be found in biographies, in letters and diaries and, more importantly, in the fiction of the period.

Keep in mind that any fictional account must be used with caution; the earlier the account, the more cautious the use. Just as all modern people do not live the kinds of lives depicted in the glitz and glamour novels, not all knights were Lancelots and Tristans nor all ladies Guineveres and Isoldes. However, one very important point about early fiction must be made. These works of the imagination depicted people *as they wished they were or wished they could be*. If you read the romances and novels of your period, you can scale down their heroes and heroines to more human characters with faults and foibles.

ONLINE SEARCHES

Much of the information I have been describing may also be obtained through electronic sources. You will need a computer (preferably a 386 or higher type), a modem (2400 baud or higher—they go up to 28,800) and a telephone line. Most new computers are fitted with modems and come with the software for several online services, such as America OnLine (AOL), Delphi and CompuServe. If not, this software is easy to obtain, often free, from many sources since the online services make their money from the monthly charges and from charges levied on special services they provide. Other online services, like GEnie, provide software that can be downloaded free or obtained from another user of that service.

The online services usually provide access to one or more electronic encyclopedias, sometimes with sound and pictures, as well as other research material. Equally, or perhaps more important, the bulletin boards hosted by such services are devoted to an enormous variety of special subjects. Among these it is possible that a request for information will bring replies from one or more experts.

More detailed information, much of it from serious scholars working in university programs, may be gleaned from the Internet. For the fearful, a good introduction is *Internet for Dummies*, by John R. Levine and Carol Baroudi. For those brave souls who want to dive right in, there is *The Internet Direct Connect Kit*, by Peter John Harrison, which not only tells you how but provides a disk of software to open the door. The shelves of any bookstore will carry dozens of other titles that will explain the how-to of getting online, and it is possible that the sales personnel of a local computer store would be able to advise.

Whether you use electronic or printed sources, you will find that one step in research leads to another. Curiosity invariably drives me far beyond the material needed for my work. I do not mind; I feel that the more I know, the more life I can give to my books because of my familiarity with the way my characters lived and thought.

RESEARCH BIBLIOGRAPHY

What follows is a basic guide to sources that might be useful to the writer of historical fiction. I have divided this bibliography into ten sections:

- Books That Tell You Where and How to Look

- Books That List Reference Books

- Bibliographies

- Dictionaries

- Encyclopedias

- Maps and Atlases

- Guides to Periodical Literature

- Series Books on History

- Biographical Sources

- Books on How People Lived

Unless specifically stated, the books within each section are not listed in any particular order. In all cases, the books mentioned are only a bare sampling of those available. They may not even be the best books on the subject. Your library may not have the particular books I mention; however, if you know such books exist and ask for them, the librarian may be able to suggest substitutes or more adequate sources. The important thing is to know that *whatever* subject you happen to be interested in, someone else was almost certainly also interested and has written and published information on that subject.

For those who have a computer and a modem, information can be retrieved from many electronic research sources (see the most recent books on research in the following section, which give directories for computer searches and a listing of information retrieval services). Data retrieval services also advertise in many computer journals; if you write or call, they will gladly send you brochures that detail their services.

Books That Tell You Where and How to Look

Barzun, Jacques, and Henry Graff. *The Modern Researcher*. Boston: Houghton Mifflin Co., 1992.

Berkman, Robert I. *Find It Fast*. New York: Harper & Row, 1987.

Clark, B., ed. *Writer's Resource Guide*. Cincinnati: Writer's Digest Books, 1983. Arranged by subject. Covers sources other than books. Better for contemporary than historical research.

Cook, M.G. *The New Library Key*. New York: H.W. Wilson, 1975. Explains library catalogs and classifications systems and how to use them; provides lists of general and special reference books with brief descriptions of contents.

Fenner, P., and M.C. Armstrong. *Research: A Practical Guide to Finding Information*. Los Altos, California: Kaufman, 1981. Explains library techniques and how to do a literature search, as well as data handling procedures for computers.

Gates, J.K. *Guide to the Use of Books and Libraries*. 3rd ed. New York: McGraw-Hill, 1974.

Horowitz, Lois. *Writer's Guide to Research*. Cincinnati: Writer's Digest Books, 1986. Slight but handy.

Morse, G.W. *Concise Guide to Library Research*. 2nd ed. New York: Fleet Academic Editions, 1975. An extensive list of reference works, listed by subject. Comparisons of what is best covered by standard reference works, such as almanacs and encyclopedias.

Todd, Alden. *Finding Facts Fast*. New York: Morrow, 1972. (Now also in paperback, $3.50.) Old but probably worth having. A useful all-around source, not nearly so detailed for library work, but of wider scope in suggesting sources other than libraries.

Books That List Reference Books

Poulton, H.J. *The Historian's Handbook: A Descriptive Guide to Reference Works*. Norman: University of Oklahoma Press, 1972.

Swidan, Eleanor A. *Reference Sources: A Brief Guide, Ninth Edition*. Baltimore: Enoch Pratt Free Library, 1988. You can own this one yourself. Current price is $7.50. Write to the Publications Department at 400 Cathedral St., Baltimore, Maryland 21201-4484. Enclose payment.

Walford, A.J. *The Guide to Reference Material*. Various eds. and supplements. London: The Library Association. Like Winchell, below, but concentrates on British books.

Winchell, C.M. *Guide to Reference*. Various eds. and supplements. Chicago: American Library Association, 1902-1986. Lists books by subject with brief descriptions of content. Concentrates on American books.

Bibliographies

Bibliographies list books in a particular subject area. There are many bibliographies; therefore, several bibliographies of bibliographies have been published. Two of these will be listed before those subject bibliographies likely to be useful to a historical novelist. This list is *far* from exhaustive. There are many useful bibliographies not listed.

American Historical Association. *Guide to Historical Literature*. New York: Macmillan, 1961.

Beers, H.P. *Bibliographies in American History*. New York: Pageant Books, 1960. Has monographs and manuscript material.

Besterman, T. *World Bibliography of Bibliographies*. Various eds. and publishers. Most comprehensive. Books listed by subject.

The Bibliographical Index. New York: Wilson, 1937-96. Lists bibliographies in books, pamphlets and periodicals.

Bibliography of British History. Vol. 1, Tudor period; Vol. 2, Stuart period; Vol. 3, eighteenth century. Oxford: Oxford University Press, 1928. Possibly other volumes by now.

Gale Research Co. *Biographical Dictionaries and Related Works: A Bibliography*. Detroit: Gale Research Co., 1967. Covers nineteenth- and twentieth-century publications.

Hammer, P.M., ed. *Guide to Archives and Manuscripts in the United States*. New Haven: Yale University Press, 1960.

Milne, A.T., ed. *Writings on British History*. New York: Barnes & Noble, 1937-61.

Dictionaries

Dictionaries are not only for definitions of words. There are dictionaries on every conceivable—and some inconceivable—subjects. A few of those most likely to be useful to the historical novelist are listed.

First are "language" dictionaries. These also contain a wide variety of factual material. If you want to know the date of an important person's birth or death, when a word was first used, simple facts about flags or coinage, the date of a saint's day, etc., look it up first in the dictionary; you will often save time.

Funk & Wagnalls New Standard Dictionary of the English Language. Biographical and geographical information included in alphabetical listings.

The Oxford English Dictionary. 12 vols. and supplements. This is best for etymology (where a word comes from) and when it was first used. There is an abridged one-volume edition that I find useful; there is also an unabridged two-volume edition, with which a magnifying glass is provided. I go to the library and use the twelve-volume edition.

Webster's International Dictionary of the English Language. I prefer the second edition (and you can get it new for about twenty dollars). Separate biographical and geographical lists.

The following list is of "special" dictionaries that might prove useful. There are many others, and the ones I list might not be best for your purposes. Check the index of the books mentioned in the first section, or ask the research librarian if you want a dictionary on a special subject.

Adams, James Truslow, ed. *Dictionary of American History.* 6 vols. New York: Scribner, 1942. There is a one-volume abridgment. This lacks the biographical sketches.

Brandon, Samuel G., ed. *Dictionary of Comparative Religion.* New York: Scribner, 1970. I have not used this. My source says "compact, covering both living and dead religions."

Eggenberger, D. *Dictionary of Battles.* New York: Crowell, 1967. Lists battles and wars by countries and chronologically.

Grose, F. *A Classical Dictionary of the Vulgar Tongue.* Ed. and commentaries by Eric Partridge. New York: Barnes & Noble, 1963. Date of original publication, 1796, says all that is necessary.

Jobes, G. *Dictionary of Mythology, Folklore, and Symbols.* 3 vols. New York: Scarecrow Press, 1961-63. All cultures, religions and civilizations from earliest recorded history to the present.

Keller, H.R. *Dictionary of Dates.* New York: Macmillan, 1934. Not in print. Arranged by countries from antiquity to 1930s.

Merriam-Webster's Biographical Dictionary. Springfield: Merriam-Webster, Inc., 1995. Contains upward of forty thousand short entries of a biographical nature.

Merriam-Webster's New Geographical Dictionary. Springfield: Merriam-Webster, Inc., 1995. Similar to the biographical dictionary but for geography.

Partridge, E. *A Dictionary of the Underworld.* New York: Bonanza Books, 1961. Argot of British and American criminals.

Partridge, E. *Slang To-day and Yesterday.* Various eds. London: Routledge; New York: Barnes & Noble. London slang.

Putnam, G.P. *Putnam's Dictionary of Events.* New York: Grosset, 1936. Arrangement chronological and parallel.

Roget's Thesaurus. Many editions, publishers and editors. This is the classic work for synonyms and has been published in dictionary form as well as the earlier style.

Spears, R.A. *Slang and Euphemism: A Dictionary.* New York: Jonathan David Publishers, 1981; New York: Signet Books, New American Library, 1982. The paperback is an abridged edition but very useful, providing many synonyms and dates of usage.

Steinberg, S.H. *Historical Tables.* Twelfth edition. New York: St. Martin's Press, 1991. I have not seen these.

Wentworth, H., and S.B. Flexner. *Dictionary of American Slang.* New York: Crowell, 1967. Dates slang.

Encyclopedias

Encyclopedias are almost as various as dictionaries. Only a few of the many available are listed here. More extensive listings can be found by consulting the "Books That Tell You Where and How to Look."

Dunan, M., ed. *Larousse Encyclopedia of Ancient and Medieval History.* New York: Harper, 1963. Not familiar with this one.

Dupuy, R. Ernest, and Trevor N. Ernest. *Encyclopedia of Military History* From 3500 B.C. to the Present. New York: Harper, 1970. Arranged chronologically and geographically.

Encyclopedia Americana. This is an excellent encyclopedia, but it has the faults of the newer *Britannica* in concentrating more on science and technology; however, it has biographical material on American historical personages and a good costume section.

Encyclopaedia Britannica. For the purposes of the historical novelist, the eleventh edition is best as it concentrates on biography, history and geography more than on scientific subjects. The ninth edition is also recommended.

Hastings, J. *Encyclopedia of Religion and Ethics.* 13 vols. New York: Scribner, 1908-27. Excellent general reference.

Langer, W.L., ed. *Encyclopedia of World History.* Boston: Houghton Mifflin, 1972. From prehistory to early 1970s.

Morris, Richard B. *Encyclopedia of American History.* New York: Harper & Row, 1970. I have not used this, but my source says, "Very good treatment. Comprehensive and authoritative."

For information on a particular religion, there are encyclopedias devoted to each well-known faith.

Maps and Atlases

A limited listing of general works only. There are atlases on almost all special areas.

Atlas of World History. Chicago: Rand McNally, 1961. Available in paperback.

McEvedy, C. *Penguin Atlas of Ancient History* and *Penguin Atlas of Medieval History*. New York: Penguin Books, 1961. Many reprints; still in print. Paperback and reasonable. Look hard for the first edition (Dutton, 1908); you won't believe the maps and descriptions.

Shepherd, W.R. *Historical Atlas*. New York: Barnes & Noble, 1964.

Treharne, R.F., and H. Fuller, ed. *Muir's Historical Atlas: Ancient, Medieval and Modern*. 2nd ed., *Atlas of Ancient and Classical History*. 9th ed., *Historical Atlas, Medieval and Modern*. New York: Barnes & Noble, 1956, 1962.

Guides to Periodical Literature

I list only two guides that deal with articles written before 1900. A guide to modern periodical literature is available in nearly every library.

Nineteenth Century Reader's Guide to Periodical Literature. 2 vols. New York: Wilson, 1994. Not complete. Intended to cover all articles from 1801 to 1899; in 1983 only 1880 to 1899 were in print and covered mostly literary articles.

Poole's Index to Periodical Literature. Reprinted by Peter Smith, 1958. Best guide. Covers 450 periodicals from 1802 to 1907.

Series Books on History

I list here only the series name. Each series contains many volumes by individual authors. Each volume is by an authoritative scholar, or scholars, in the particular period it covers and will provide a reliable and detailed study of political and social events.

Arsky, L., N. Pries, and M. Reed. *American Diaries*. Detroit: 1983. Volume 1: 2,500 published diaries written in 1492-1844. Volume 2 (not yet published): diaries of 1845-1980. List of contents annotated and arranged chronologically. Subject and geographical indexes. (Reference courtesy Hertha Schulze; not used by me.)

The Cambridge Ancient History. 12 vols. and 5 vols. plates. Cambridge: Cambridge University Press. Covers world history from prehistoric times to about A.D. 350.

The Cambridge Medieval History. 8 vols. Cambridge: Cambridge University Press. There is a condensation of this work in two volumes. World history from 350 to about 1500.

Commager, H.S. and R.B. Morris, ed. *The New American Nation.* New York: Harper, 1954-. Not complete. To be forty volumes. I am not familiar with either series on American history—not my field—but I am told the *New* series does not replace but complements the older one.

Hart, A.B., ed. *The American Nation.* 28 vols. New York: Harper, 1904-18. Ends before beginning of World War I.

The New Cambridge Modern History. 13 vols. and atlas. Cambridge: Cambridge University Press. World history 1493-1945.

The Oxford History of England. 14 vols. Oxford: Clarendon. This series is concerned with England, world history being dealt with only incidentally.

Biographical Sources

I list only biographical sources dealing with historical personages, that is, those who are dead.

Dictionary of American Biography. 20 vols. and supplements. Biographical sketches of historical American personages. The length of the biography roughly corresponds to the importance of the individual.

Dictionary of National Biography. 21 vols. and supplements. As above but for British personages.

Who's Who in History. 5 vols. Oxford: Blackwell, 1960-74. British history. I have not seen this. Use the *DNB* if you can.

Books on How People Lived

There are many specific books on each period and each country.

The Everyday Life Series. London: B.T. Batsford; New York: G.P. Putnam's. Like series books on history, this series consists of many volumes by different authors. In general, this is the most useful group of books I have come across for the historical novelist, although they are written for "young readers." The books give details of customs, costumes, food and level of technology (i.e., whether the people had horses, whether there were saddles for them, whether the wheel had already been invented in this particular society, etc.). Each volume varies in arrangement and period of time covered. Some of the volumes cover life in prehistoric times, ancient Egypt, Babylonia and Assyria, ancient Greece, Imperial China, Rome and Britain at all time periods.

Scott, A.F. *Everyone a Witness Series.* New York: Crowell. These books are anthologies of quotations from various sources written in the period defined by the title of the individual volume. The subjects of the extracts cover everything from brief biographies and descriptions of royal personages to every aspect of daily life, such as towns, wages, sports, law and crime, the arts and education. Individual volumes are titled *The Plantagenet Age*, *The Tudor Age*, *The Stuart Age*, *The Norman Age*, *The Edwardian Age*.

Here is a limited list of books on costume and food for those who are curious or would like more details. Many books on each subject are available.

Costume

Braun and Schneider. *Historic Costume in Pictures.* New York: Dover Publications. A black-and-white picture book, but the illustrations are clear and detailed, better than Laver. Can be ordered from Dover ($7.50) so you can have this one at home.

Costume Index. New York: Wilson, 1937, 1957. Locates plates and pictures of costumes in books. Covers almost all historical periods and all nations.

Davenport, M. *The Book of Costume.* 2 vols. New York: Crown, 1948. All illustrations are reproductions of sculpture or paintings and sometimes difficult to make out. The text is very detailed.

Hiler, H. *Bibliography of Costume.* New York: Wilson, 1939. I have not used this work, but bibliographies are always useful.

Laver, J. *Costume Through the Ages*. New York: Simon & Schuster, 1963. Essentially a picture book, black and white; no text.

Mansfield, A. *Ceremonial Costume Court, Civil & Civic Costume From Sixteen Sixty to the Present Day*. Lanham: Barnes & Noble, 1980. English ceremonial dress.

Sichel, M. *Costume Reference*. 7 vols. Boston: Plays, Inc., 1977. British costume only. Slim volumes but excellent.

Wilcox, R.T. *Dictionary of Costume*. New York: Scribner, 1969.

Worrell, E.A. *Early American Costume*. Harrisburg, PA: Stackpole Books, 1975. Covers 1580-1850. Illustrations drawn and accompanied directly by limited text.

Yarwood, D. *Encyclopedia of World Costume*. Scribner, 1978. Reprint, New York: Bonanza Books. References in alphabetical order rather than chronological order, e.g., *hat* gives history and several pages of illustrations. Useful if you know the name of an item and are not sure when it appeared. Index gives cross-references.

Yarwood, D. *European Costume*. New York: Larousse, 1975. Useful but not very detailed.

Food and Drink

I have never seen the first two books, but they were the only general references I could find in English. The others are books I have used because they were available, not because they were most complete or best.

Bitting, K.G. *Gastronomic Bibliography*. San Francisco, 1939.

Food and Drink Through the Ages. London: Maggs Bros. Catalog of books on this subject through 1937.

Clair, C. *Kitchen and Table*. New York: Abelard-Schuman, 1965. Covers primitive to Victorian times with special sections on table settings, drinking vessels, the evolution of the kitchen and four notable cooks.

Cosman, M.P. *Fabulous Feasts: Medieval Cookery and Ceremony*. New York: George Braziller, 1976. Exquisite color plates, good text, but rather expensive ($25).

Driver, C., and M. Berriedale-Johnson. *Pepys at Table*. Berkeley and Los Angeles: University of California Press, 1984. A complete and utter delight. Little extracts from Pepys's diary, songs, delightful comments and illustrations. A must for anyone with an interest in the seventeenth century.

Kuper, J., ed. *The Anthropologists' Cookbook*. New York: Universe, 1977. Not a historical text, but it does contain recipes from areas seldom included in ordinary cookbooks and using unusual ingredients, such as puffins, wild greens and dogs. Each chapter has an introductory text that gives a brief glance at eating habits in odd places.

Pullar, P. *Consuming Passions*. Boston: Little, Brown, 1970. A violently caustic history of food and eating habits from Roman times to the present. Pullar doesn't like anyone, but the book has lots of information. It may give you high blood pressure, but it's fun to read.

Quayle, E. *Old Cook Books*. New York: Dutton, 1978. Many illustrations and actual recipes.

Sass, L.J. *To the King's Taste: Richard II's Book of Feasts and Recipes*. You can make these if you like; they are translated and adapted for modern cooking, but the old recipes and language (with explanations) are given too.

Simmons, Amelia. *American Cookery 1796*. Facsimile copy, *The First American Cookbook*. New York: Oxford University Press, 1958. Reprint, New York: Dover, 1984. The original date says it all. It's a little hard to read, but it's fun, and there is an interesting introduction with a good bibliography by Mary Tolford Wilson.

Tannahill, Reay. *Food in History*. New York: Stein & Day, 1973. A broad study of how food affected history and how history affected food.

Libraries and Special Libraries

American Library Directory. New Providence: R.R. Bowker, annual publication.

Directory of Special Libraries and Information Centers. 3rd ed. 3 vols. Gale Research Co., 1974.

Subject Collections: A Guide to Special Libraries. 4th ed. R.R. Bowker, 1974.

World Guide to Libraries. 4th ed. 2 vols. R.R. Bowker, 1974.

There are now more recent editions of most of the above books, and these are likely to be available in your library.

CHAPTER 13

Point of View—His? Hers? How Many?

Glenda Sanders

Point of view (POV) may be the least discussed element of fiction writing, but, used effectively, it is a powerful tool capable of influencing every aspect of a story, from characterization to conflict, plot to pacing.

The term *point of view* is self defining. Simply put, the writer decides from whose point of view a scene would be told with the most impact and writes from that character's perspective.

Literary conventions regarding POV are constantly changing. Once any change of POV within a chapter was frowned upon as amateurish; now such changes are common, with restrictions (if rigidly enforced) on scenes instead of chapters. It is not uncommon in today's romance novels to find the POV of both lead characters within a single scene.

Early romance novels were written exclusively in the heroine's POV. Readers observed the world through her eyes, heard it through her ears and reacted to her personal experience. The hero was usually presented as a total mystery to her, often brooding and overbearing. Although the reader could anticipate a happy resolution, the hero's declaration of love at the end of the book frequently came as a total surprise to the heroine.

As the genre grew up and heroines became more mature, more sophisticated and increasingly self-confident, surprise declarations no longer rang true to readers. Books grew longer and stories more complex. Writers experimented with adding the hero's POV to add dimension to the longer stories, and the technique proved practical for the purposes of storytelling as well as popular with readers.

OMNISCIENT NARRATION VS. CHARACTER VIEWPOINT

Omniscient narration is storytelling from an all-seeing, all-knowing perspective. An omniscient narrator is much like the storyteller of old, relating a fairy tale from beginning to end. She knows the entire story and may interject phrases such as, "The princess would never have agreed to marry the ogre if she had known the prince was alive and waiting for her around the next curve in the road."

With character POV, a writer shows the reader the story events through the eyes, ears and individual perceptions of a character, limiting what is revealed to what the viewpoint character is seeing, hearing and feeling. Some writers say they put an imaginary camera with video and audio receptors on the viewpoint character's head, and then report what the camera picks up. Instead of merely being told a story, the reader experiences it along with the character.

Notice that I said an omniscient narrator *tells* and a POV writer *shows*. This is an important distinction. A reader may be drawn into a story she is told, but she is more likely to *feel* a story she is shown. Since emotion is the central focus of a romance novel, POV narration is highly favored over omniscient narration.

Because omniscient narration puts an emotional buffer between the reader and the character, it should be used with discretion, when the writer wishes to convey necessary but not necessarily emotionally engaging information to the reader quickly and with an economy of words.

CHARACTER POV—BUT WHOSE?

A couple who attend a fashion show or visit a hardware store together will give different "reviews" of the event. Asked to report on the fashion show, a woman might comment on changing trends in skirt lengths, use of accessories and which colors are "hot," while her husband recalls a certain garment that showed a model's legs or bosom to advantage. The woman might find the hardware store dusty and its to-the-ceiling shelves daunting, while her husband is enraptured by the bins of wing nuts and electrical connectors.

Almost any story event will be perceived differently by each character involved. Sometimes the differences in perception are subtle, sometimes dramatic. A skillful writer will decide which perspective is most useful to the story he is telling.

You may find these questions useful in deciding which POV is appropriate to a particular scene:

- Why is this scene important to the story? What do I hope to achieve by including it in the story?

- How would each character perceive this situation?

- Which perspective would be most useful to the story?

USING POINT OF VIEW TO STRENGTHEN CHARACTERIZATION

Used effectively, character POV provides a unique glimpse into a character's mind and perspectives, building a strong and intimate rapport between the reader and the character. By reacting to the scene along with the character, the reader learns much about the character's history and background. Does she hum along with Bach? Mozart? Hootie and the Blowfish? Does she recognize work by Monet or simply think a picture is beautiful? Does she compare a handsome man to Cary Grant, Sean Connery or Keanu Reeves? Does she compare a delicate dessert to Godiva chocolate or a Hershey's Kiss?

A skillful writer will use detail to characterize through POV as the story progresses. Compare these two approaches to a woman who looks at a piece of silver flatware.

Omniscient POV: *She noticed that the table was set with Grande Baroque by Wallace.*

Character POV: *Grand Baroque. Theresa bit back a wry smile as she traced the ornate knife handle with her fingertip. She'd always loved the pattern, but Charles had talked her out of buying it because he considered it ostentatious. She should have bought the Grand Baroque and told Charles to take a hike; it would have saved the trouble of divorcing him five years down the road.*

POINT OF VIEW HEIGHTENS STORY CONFLICT

Conflict is important to the story only to the extent that it is important to your characters. By using POV to allow the reader an intimate glimpse inside the character's perspectives, the writer allows the reader to understand why the character is threatened by the conflict and why she feels so strongly about the subject. This is particularly effective when the reader is given the perspectives of both characters so that the reader, caring about both characters and wanting each to be happy, is drawn into the conflict.

Example: Kelly and Tom are lovers, very much in love. Tom is offered a big promotion in Colorado.

The author could introduce the conflict through omniscient narration: *Tom, an avid skier and outdoorsman, had been trying to get to Colorado all his adult life; for him this promotion and relocation was a dream come true. But Kelly refused to go with him. She appreciated her job at the bank too much to give it up easily, and she could not leave her sister, Diedre, to face the last, painful stages of ovarian cancer alone.*

Compare the above treatment to the POV narrative, which draws the reader more intimately into the emotional upheaval in the conflict situation.

Tom: *Colorado! Ski slopes. Hiking trails. Mountain air. And the new managership would give him the money to enjoy it all—with Kelly. If Tom had tried to write a memo describing his dream job and his dream life, he'd have written that he would meet a woman like Kelly then get offered a great job in Colorado.*

Kelly: *Colorado. Kelly's heart sank as Tom talked on, painting vivid word pictures of the fun they would have exploring the mountains together. More than anything in the world, she wanted to throw her arms around him and tell him how thrilled she was to be going with him. But she couldn't. Not when Diedre was so weak and scared.*

This intimate glimpse into Tom's thought processes and similar glimpse into Kelly's perspective help us anticipate Tom's disappointment when Kelly refuses to move to Colorado with him and shows us Kelly's internal turmoil over having to disappoint him. And because we empathize with both characters, we are drawn into the conflict and frustration they feel.

POINT OF VIEW BUILDS SUSPENSE

By controlling the information available to the reader, an author can use POV to build suspense. Perhaps the most obvious examples of this use of POV were the classic gothic romances, which dropped an innocent heroine into a dark and menacing setting, often a spooky old house. These tales were traditionally told in the first person, which meant that the reader saw the world through the eyes of the heroine and heard it through her ears. While the first person narration and conversational tone in which these stories were told established an instant rapport between the heroine and the reader, the limited information the reader was given enabled the author to make all the remaining characters, from the mysterious hero to his seemingly genteel great aunt, suspect.

While first person is largely out of favor with readers now, writers may use limited viewpoint within a scene to generate suspense, often by alternating between points of view in order to give the reader information the lead character does not have. For instance, a brief scene in a stalker's POV will alert the reader that the heroine is being stalked, thus keeping the reader gritting her teeth wanting to warn the heroine while the heroine obliviously goes about her normal routine.

In a romance, the hero's POV is often used the same way. The reader knows the hero is trustworthy because she is shown his introspection, but the heroine does not know she can trust him. The reader grits her teeth, willing the heroine to trust the hero so the story can be resolved.

Another effective technique is controlling information within a POV—giving the reader enough information to suggest but not confirm. In my Harlequin Temptation *Look Into My Eyes*, the hero claimed to have amnesia, but the heroine was warned that he might be a con artist. By giving the reader his feelings about the heroine without delving into the emotionality of his memory loss in his POV, I kept the reader guessing whether the hero was telling the truth or running a scam. He expressed his bewilderment and frustration over his situation when talking to the heroine in scenes in her POV, but the reader, along with the heroine, had to decide whether the hero was sincere.

POINT OF VIEW AND PACING

Generally, omniscient narration is used to convey relevant information or establish a setting very quickly when the information or setting is not crucial to the plot. In other words, when the reader needs to know where the characters are but the setting holds no particular significance to the characters or action.

Three months later, they ran into each other at the corner supermarket. This phrase of omniscient narration efficiently tells the reader how much time has passed since the previous scene and where the characters happened to meet. We can assume that the supermarket provides a backdrop for the action but is not emotionally significant to either character.

Contrast that treatment with this: *Three months went by before Sara was able to go back into the supermarket.*

She was immediately struck by how normal everything seemed. Shoppers pushed carts with squeaking wheels between long rows of merchandise, plucking breakfast cereals, cat food, canned vegetables and toothpaste from the shelves, oblivious to the fact that a woman had been gunned down while browsing the same shelves.

Closing her eyes to blink back the image of Mrs. Barker sprawled on the tile floor in a widening pool of blood, Sara opened them seconds later to see a familiar figure walking her way. She recognized the broad shoulders and graceful gait immediately. Ronald. What had brought him back to the scene of the crime? Had it drawn him the way it had drawn her?

POINT OF VIEW PITFALLS
Omniscient Narration and Author Intrusion

When a writer interjects opinion or violates point of view in order to give the reader information that the characters would not logically know through events within the action of the story, this is referred to as *author intrusion.*

Kelly didn't know going to Colorado was so important to Tom, although she should have. (Omniscient Point of View/Telling/ Intrusive)

Contrast that treatment with this: *The horrible scene with Tom kept running through Kelly's mind. She hadn't realized how badly he'd wanted to move to Colorado until she'd seen the fire of enthusiasm in his eyes as he'd spoken of hiking through the mountain trails together.* (Character Point of View/Showing)

Mind Hopping

While literary conventions have eased, allowing writers to shift from one character's POV to another's within a scene, moving from one POV to the other requires skill. The author, when writing, and the reader, when reading, must know beyond any doubt from whose point of view a scene or, in some cases, a paragraph is being shown.

Abrupt POV shifts quickly become confusing or tiresome. A reader mustn't feel as though she's figuratively twisting her head back and forth from one character's head to the other. Therefore, a writer should change POV only when showing the multiple POV within a scene to strengthen the emotional impact of a story.

Generally speaking, scenes of strong conflict and scenes in which the hero and heroine make love, both of which rely on strong emotional involvement of the characters and the readers for their success, benefit most from frequent POV changes. POV shifts are more common in these scenes than any other and can be quite effective—as long as the writer makes sure the reader knows which character's head she's in. When a reader has to stop and read a sentence over for any reason, including to double-check who is thinking or speaking, the writer risks losing that reader.

PRACTICE MAKES PERFECT

POV is a valuable writer's tool. Used properly, it draws the reader into the emotion of the story. Abused or used inappropriately, it weakens a story and confuses a reader. And like any tool in any trade, it is most efficiently used after extensive practice.

If you are having trouble with a scene and suspect your problem might be related to character POV, try writing the scene in the first-person narrative from the viewpoint of each character involved. Include thoughts and impressions. Then compare the different versions, evaluating each in terms of how valuable that particular perspective would be to the story you are telling. Using your first-person account as a guide, rewrite the scene in third person, from the POV of the character whose POV you have deemed most valuable to your story.

CHAPTER 14

Aiming for the Goal

Karen Robards

Health, wealth, the pursuit of happiness: These are some of the goals I keep chasing through life. They are probably high on your list of goals, too. If, as a writer, you create fictional characters, your creations likely want pretty much the same things you and I do. After all, our goal as writers is to make our characters seem no less real than any other denizen of this planet. Think of it this way: We're not writing fiction; we're giving birth to paper people. Since goals motivate behavior, defining our characters' goals is a way for us to make them come alive. Each of your characters need goals, even your minor ones and your villains. And just as every action has a reaction, every action in fiction should have a goal.

DETERMINING CHARACTER GOALS: A CASE STUDY

I'm going to use one of my books, *Walking After Midnight*, as an illustration. Assuming (hoping?) that everyone who reads this article has read the book would probably be assuming too much, so let me give you a thumbnail description of the plot:

Summer, my heroine, while scrubbing the bathroom of a funeral home, encounters a not-quite-dead corpse (Steve) who kidnaps her and takes her with him as he runs for his life.

OK, let's take that premise apart: What are the characters' goals in this book?

Steve is running for his life. His goal is to stay alive. As he becomes more involved with Summer, his goal expands to include keeping her alive, too.

This goal of staying alive is the engine of the book. It is the force that propels the action. It is the *primary goal*.

Every work of fiction and every character need a primary goal.

Steve has secondary goals as well: to find out who wants to kill him and why; to solve the riddle of the suicide of his former lover, for which he was blamed; to make up to his teenage daughter for not being the father he should have been to her; to regain his self-respect.

As the plot unfolds, he develops additional secondary goals: to develop a relationship with Summer and to rid himself of DeeDee, the aforementioned former lover whose ghost keeps popping up at the most inconvenient moments.

All Steve's actions, from being in the funeral home in the first place to buying a puppy for his daughter, are in pursuit of a goal.

Summer has goals, too: Like Steve, her primary goal is to stay alive. Her secondary goals include going home. They include keeping Muffy, her mother's prize Pekinese, out of the hands of the bad guys. They include, at first, escaping from Steve. When she realizes that her fate is inextricably bound to his, this secondary goal changes to helping Steve to realize *his* goals so they can both live long enough to reach the happily ever after at the end of the book.

Goals (even, sometimes, the primary goal) can change as circumstances and characters do. Secondary goals can enter or leave a story at just about any point. Muffy does not enter barking until approximately a third of the way into *Walking After Midnight*. Obviously, Summer's goal of keeping Muffy safe cannot enter before the dog does. In addition, Muffy's life-or-death predicament is resolved before Summer and Steve's. This secondary goal is met, while leaving the primary goal intact to continue to fuel the book.

Third in importance after the primary and the secondary goals are the periphery goals, or goals not essential to the main thrust of the action but nonetheless essential to the believability of the book. Let's call them the whys.

Why is Summer scrubbing the bathroom of the funeral home where she first encounters Steve? Because she owns Daisy Fresh, a cleaning service, and the funeral home is one of her biggest clients. Her goal in being in that funeral home at that particular time (the middle of the night) is to build her business, please her customer, make money. *This goal gives her a legitimate reason to be where she is.*

(FYI, I consider coincidence the bane of good fiction, whether I'm reading it or writing it. Give me a good, goal-based reason for something happening every time.)

Why does Summer investigate the moving "corpse" in the embalming room herself, rather than calling the police (or whomever) to do it? See the above-mentioned goal of building her business and pleasing her customer. (If *you* were a fledgling business owner, would you call your most important client at 2 A.M. and tell him one of his corpses wasn't dead unless you were darn sure of it? See how putting yourself in your main character's shoes—identifying with her goals—helps move the plot along?)

Why does Summer take Muffy with her as she runs for her life? Because Summer is dog-sitting (the dog belongs to her mother, who is traveling), and Muffy is in the house when Summer encounters the villains there. (Actually, Muffy aids in Summer and Steve's escape.) Summer's goal is to keep Muffy out of the hands of the bad guys. A comic foil is thus added to the book *for a very good reason.*

Why does Steve kidnap Summer? Because he means to use her as a hostage and a driver to realize his goal of escape.

Why does Steve need Summer as a hostage and a driver? He needs a hostage because bad guys are trying to kill him, and he initially thinks Summer is one of the bad guys. He needs a driver because he can't see to drive, a result of the injuries that put him into his near-corpselike state in the first place.

Why does Steve keep Summer with him once he is clear of the funeral home and no longer needs either a hostage or a driver? Because he feels responsible for having gotten her involved in something that might cost her her life. Remember Steve's expanded goal of keeping Summer alive?

Just in case I haven't motivated you to rush right out and buy a copy of *Walking After Midnight*, let's try this on a slightly more widely read work of fiction: *Gone With The Wind*. (You haven't read that either? Get busy. No writer ever wrote anything publishable without being an avid reader first.)

What was Scarlett's primary goal? To get Ashley Wilkes. This was the engine that drove that book.

She had lots of secondary goals (collect as many men as she could, save Tara) and periphery goals (dance at that party while she was still in mourning for her first husband). They added color and readability to the book, moving the action from point A to point B.

But Scarlett's relentless pursuit of Ashley was what got us all the way from A to Z.

DEFINING THE PRIMARY GOAL

Determining your characters' goals can be a great aid in plotting your book. First, of course, you want to define the primary goal.

To do this, it helps to write the premise of your book as briefly as possible, preferably in one sentence. Look at what you wrote, then ask yourself, What does your main character want most?

It might be to live. It might be a man. It might be to win the Pillsbury Bake-Off. But this is your primary goal. This is the engine driving your book.

Every action (goal) stems from your characters' pursuit of the primary goal.

Try putting your story's goals in outline form. Write the primary goal as the main heading. List the secondary goals as points A and B under the main heading. Add the periphery goals (the whys) as the numbered points under A and B.

As you work on your novel, remember that constantly aiming toward the realization of your characters' primary goal is the fiction writer's equivalent of keeping your eye on the ball. Secondary goals motivate secondary (but still important) actions. Periphery goals are the whys behind everday actions. Goals can change as your characters and situations do. New goals can appear along the way.

Think of goals as skeletons on which to hang the flesh of a story. Think of goals as slopes to be scaled on the way to conquering the peak of Mt. Everest.

Realizing the primary goal is like making it to your book's promised land. When you get there, you are done.

Except for a brief wrap-up, maybe. The epilogue. The fading into the sunset. The final kiss. You know what I mean.

The happily ever after. Which, by the way, you might want to think of as the ultimate primary goal.

CHAPTER 15

The Art of Keeping the Reader Reading

Linda Barlow

There is nothing as important to a writer's success as his ability to hook his readers and keep them turning the pages. When a reader says to me, "I loved your book. I couldn't put it down," I know I've done my job well. If she was so compelled by my story that she put aside her other tasks until she finished it, chances are high that she will rush out to buy my next book. As long as I continue to write compelling stories that grab her attention and hold it until the final page, I will have a loyal and devoted fan.

Compelling readers to keep reading is important at every step of the bookselling process, beginning when your manuscript goes out to the first agent or editor you've contacted. Ideally, an editor will become so involved in reading the manuscript you submitted that he'll lock his office door and let his answering machine take all his calls. You want him to present your book at his next editorial acquisition meeting with the rousing recommendation "I couldn't put it down."

CREATING SUSPENSE

In order to hook your readers and keep their undivided attention, you must create suspense, which is one of the essential ingredients of all great storytelling. A wonderful storyteller has her reader at her mercy. While you are engaged in reading one of her books, it becomes the most important thing in your life: You empathize with the main characters, feeling their emotions as if they were your own; you stay up until 2 A.M. avidly turning the pages; and when you finally get to the last page, you feel that odd combination of elation and sadness—elation because things have worked out exactly the way they were supposed to work out and sadness because your wonderful reading experience is over.

How does a great romantic storyteller keep her readers reading?

She builds suspense by creating sympathetic characters and confronting them with a series of plot complications. As readers watch the characters they care about getting plunged into conflict or trouble, the hope that the hero and heroine will prevail is coupled with a fear that they might not. This tension between hope and fear creates suspense, and readers feel compelled to keep turning the pages until they know how it's all going to turn out.

The romance novel presents a special challenge in this regard, however. In a romance, the readers already *know* the ending. The hero and heroine are going to resolve their problems and live happily ever after. This, after all, is the traditional ending of all romances.

Almost from the beginning, as hero and heroine catch each other's eye and feel the powerful attraction that is drawing them together, your alert romance fan/reader knows that these two are meant for each other. Deep in their hearts, the hero and heroine know it, too. But if being meant for each other was all there was to it, you wouldn't have a story at all. You—and your reader—might as well skip directly to the last page.

A romance is not just a love story; it's a love story with obstacles. Your hero and heroine are going to have to earn that happy ending, and those obstacles should create the necessary suspense.

BUILDING YOUR PLOT

The plot of any novel, no matter what the genre, should enmesh the protagonists in a series of escalating conflicts leading toward a dramatic climax. The plot may be simple or it may be so complex that its resolution involves the unraveling of many separately wound threads, but romances tend to be more straightforwardly plotted than mystery or suspense novels.

The main plot of a romance always concerns the romantic relationship itself. I feel I must repeat that sentence since it is crucial to understanding the structure of a romance: *The main plot of a romance always concerns the romantic relationship itself.*

Or, to put it another way (with apologies to the 1992 Presidential campaign): *It's the relationship, stupid.*

What do I mean by this? Simply that the love story between the hero and the heroine is the most important story you're telling. Don't ever forget that! Depending on the length and form of a romance novel, you might be telling other stories. You might have a subplot about the villain's attempts to destroy the corporation the hero runs. But if you are writing a true romance novel (as opposed to a romantic suspense novel or a romantic mystery), such subplots will never overwhelm the main plot. You must keep the relationship between the hero and the heroine central. Strong subplots and memorable minor characters are wonderful additions to a novel, but no one is more important to your readers than your hero and heroine. It is in the main plot that the author should invest most of her emotional and creative energy. The relationship *is* the story.

If the hero and heroine are meant for each other, what's going to happen to keep them from falling immediately into each other's arms and declaring their undying love? That is a key question you must ask yourself as you begin plotting your novel. Although romances focus on the process by which a man and a woman come together and fall in love, you'll need to give serious thought to the things that are going to keep them apart.

And for that, you need conflict.

Conflict, in fact, is one of the most essential ingredients of any story.

What exactly *is* conflict?

Essentially, a conflict is a complication that causes a problem between two or more characters. Conflicts are those bumps on the road that prevent the course of true love from running smooth.

For example: Suppose you are writing a historical romance set during the American Civil War. Your heroine is a Confederate lady trying to defend what remains of her plantation after her father and her brothers have been killed in the war. Your hero is a Union officer who is seeking a place to quarter his hungry, battle-weary troop of soldiers. Your hero and heroine meet and feel the pull of that eternal mystery—love. But they are enemies, and the conflict between love and honor is bound to cause them much suffering and anguish.

Although this is a dramatic example, the notion of the hero and the heroine as loving enemies is a useful way to look at the plot structure of a great many romances. The classic paradigm in romance is that the relationship between the hero and heroine is almost always paradoxical: He is her bitterest enemy, yet still they love. She represents the greatest possible threat to his peace of mind, yet still they love. She fears him, yet still they love. He wants revenge on her family, yet still they love.

Why do the conflicts in romances tend to be so melodramatic? Because the familiar plot elements we use in romance derive from ancient legends and myths, and many of these myths reflect a fundamental, age-old truth about human relations: that men and women don't understand each other very well. The age-old battle of the sexes is continually played out in these romantic stories: The heroes usually strive to maintain male ideals of autonomy and independence, while the heroines yearn for intimacy and bonding. Male and female are eternally at odds with each other, but they are fused by the miraculous power of love. *Love conquers all* is the essence of romance.

But remember, love doesn't conquer all *easily*. One of the most common mistakes I see in the manuscripts of aspiring romance novelists is the lack of sustained conflict. Most writers are pretty good at setting up an initial conflict between their hero and heroine, but they don't seem to know how to build on initial conflict. While it may be the initial conflict that will entice an agent or an editor to start reading your manuscript, it is your ability to build the suspense and intensify the conflict that will keep him turning the pages.

Therefore, you need a series of complications that grow more and more dramatic as the plot advances. The first conflict should change the status quo and place the hero and heroine in an entirely new situation. As they struggle to deal with that, a new, more difficult conflict arises, causing new complications and new changes. And thus the story progresses—situation, conflict, change, situation, conflict, change. The protagonists in a good, solid story will develop as characters as a result of the conflicts they face. This character development is important because it will often help them in some way at the novel's climactic point, when they must confront the most difficult challenge of all.

In my historical romance *Fires of Destiny*, Alexandra, my heroine, realizes she is in love with the hero, Roger, when he returns home after several years away. The first conflict is simple: He doesn't love her back. Undaunted, she sets out to be as engaging as possible and to prove to him that she is a woman, not the child he remembers. But a more serious conflict quickly arises: Just as he does begin to feel an interest in her, she finds reason to suspect him of murder. Her suspicion sets off a chain of events that leads to their being separated just as the passion is heating up on both sides.

Forbidden to see each other, Roger and Alexandra find themselves on opposing sides of the religious/political spectrum in the court of Queen Mary Tudor. Through their own mistakes and the treachery of their enemies, Roger comes to believe Alexandra has betrayed him, causing a violent confrontation that nearly kills them both. Once *that* mess is cleared up, they are briefly happy with each other before the next complication ensues. And so it goes, one complication after another until they face the most difficult of all: Roger is caught and imprisoned in the Tower of London, condemned to death for treason and heresy. This is the point where Alexandra must use everything she has learned in the course of the story if she's going to save her lover and achieve their happy ending.

A tip to remember when building conflict is that you should never resolve one complication without having already introduced the next. You don't want the reader to think, "Whew, they finally solved that problem. Now everything will be OK." She might stop reading! Instead you want her to think, "Well, I'm glad that's cleared up, but, my goodness, how are they going to get out of *this?*"

Remember that in any long narrative there are natural points where the action winds down a bit, at the end of a chapter, for example. Although I'm not averse to granting the reader *some* respite now and then, I prefer to end chapters with some sort of cliff-hanger that forces readers to keep turning those pages. Since readers feel, psychologically, that they're supposed to pause at the end of a chapter, being unable to do so makes them feel they are reading an exciting and compelling story.

TYPES OF CONFLICT

Fires of Destiny made frequent use of external conflict to separate the lovers, e.g., the political situation, the treacheries of other people, even the well-meaning actions of friends. External conflicts provide excitement, adventure and interesting plot twists, but it's wise to mix external conflicts with internal ones, since it's the internal, psychological conflicts that provide the real emotional power in a novel.

Internal conflict takes place in the character's head. In *Fires of Destiny*, Roger's inner conflict concerns his deep-seated guilt over several past events in his life. He believes himself to be a poor candidate for marriage, and his essentially honorable nature prevents him from offering himself to Alexandra, the woman he comes to love, because he's afraid he'll screw up her life.

It would be difficult to find a good romance novel that didn't include several powerful psychological conflicts. Some examples that come to mind include the hero who is bitter about love and has sworn never to trust another woman. Or the heroine who has been abused by a former lover and is torn between her attraction to the hero and her inner fear that he, too, might prove to be abusive toward her. There are endless possibilities, and a good writer will find and exploit some of them because it is vitally important to make an emotional connection with your readers. Ideally, you want them to *feel* as they read—to laugh, to get worried, to get angry, to cry. If your characters are passionate enough to feel authentic human emotions, your readers will empathize and feel them, too.

Emotional conflicts touch the hearts of readers because everyone can relate to at least some of these intense emotions. We can also relate to the anguish that fictional characters experience while trying to resolve internal conflicts. We all have problems in our relationships. We all find it hard to work things out with certain people in our lives, whether they be parents, children, friends, professional acquaintances or lovers. Love, because it is so powerful, forces the hero and heroine to resolve their emotional doubts, fears and confusions, and this reminds the reader that love does indeed have the power to heal in real life as well.

SATISFYING ENDINGS

Great storytellers not only raise the expectations of their readers, they also satisfy them. The endings of their novels *work*.

How do you pull off a convincing happy ending? You must both surprise and delight your readers. In other words, your ending should, in some way, be surprising, yet, at the same time, it must also be the only possible ending that fits everything you have revealed about the characters and their emotions. Your hero and heroine should come together in harmony and mutual love because they have resolved their conflicts in a creative way and in the only way that could ever have been possible for them.

Only then will your reader close your book with a smile on her face, satisfied that in this case, the happily-ever-after ending is well deserved.

CHAPTER 16

Secrets for Creating a Best-Selling Romance

Jude Deveraux

In the twelve years since I was first published, I've read a number of romances that were beautifully written, exhaustively researched, but that ultimately, when published, didn't sell. Since I'm the type of person who analyzes everything, I've tried to figure out just what it is about these books that made them fail to capture the imaginations of the readers.

There are hard-and-fast rules to writing a romance, rules that cannot be broken and boundaries that must not be crossed. For instance, you can put a mystery in your romance, but if you put in even a bit too much mystery, you have a book that won't be bought by either mystery readers or romance readers.

Here are nine other common problems I have seen both in unpublished manuscripts and in published books that didn't find an audience.

DON'T GIVE YOUR CHARACTERS TOO MANY PERSONALITY TRAITS

It's natural to want to put everything admirable into your hero or heroine. Since your heroine is usually your main character, you will probably want her to be all the good things a person can be. You'll want her to be noble and brave, a lover of children and animals, well educated, a bit persecuted by others (so readers will feel a tug at their heartstrings), spunky, desired by the best of the men and so on.

Unfortunately, when you assign this whole list of attributes to one person, you don't end up with a noble, bigger-than-life character; you create a mess no one can identify with.

For example, let's say you open your book with a scene in which the heroine is being unfairly accused of something by the villainess, then follow with a scene in which the heroine sees a child crying, then show the heroine finding out that the child is crying because her kitten is stuck up in a tree, then have your heroine risking her life to rescue the kitten, then let the heroine fall out of the tree into the hero's arms, then make the heroine lash out at him for daring to look at her in "that way." What you have is a hodge-podge of personality traits. Readers are going to have no idea what the character you've created is really like. Pick out one or two personality traits, and stick with them throughout the novel. You can, for example, write a whole book on a heroine who is, first and foremost, a lover of children.

DON'T MISTAKE CLICHÉS FOR PLOT

By clichés I mean plot lines that have been used over and over in fiction. For example, years ago I read a romance that was absolutely cliché ridden. When I bought that author's next book, I looked at the back cover just enough to see that it was set on a riverboat. I made a list of all the clichés about riverboat romances I could think of: Either the villain or the hero was going to be a riverboat gambler and wear a gold brocade vest. There was going to be a fire or a riverboat race. Samuel Clemens was going to be the pilot of the boat, and they'd dock in New Orleans. There'd be some hanky-panky in the brothels of New Orleans. I wrote an entire page of clichés.

After I'd made my list, I read the book. *All* of the clichés on my list were there (in fact, *both* the hero and the villain were gamblers wearing gold brocade vests). Today this author cannot find a publisher for her books.

Sometimes, as I write, I come up with scenes just by thinking of what one would predict a romance character might do and then writing something as close to the cliché's opposite as I can make it.

AVOID ADORED/PERSECUTED HEROINES

This is the most difficult problem to explain to new romance writers. In some manuscripts, every character in the book either loves the heroine or hates her, and by the end of the book, the people who have not fallen in love with her (and this includes servants) are killed off by the author in proportionately vicious ways. In some books, this is carried so far that everyone—main characters, minor characters all—are able to put themselves in the heroine's lovely little mind and sense whatever she's feeling.

Instead of having your heroine be the center of *everyone's* universe, make her liked by some, disliked by others and ignored by the rest.

DON'T OVERDO THE SEX

Romance novels are not sex novels. They are books about people learning about each other and falling in love. Sex is a tiny part of love, but too often the whole "story" of a beginner's romance novel is nothing but a never-ending sex scene. If the heroine leaves her house, some man is going to try to rape her. If the heroine climbs a ladder, she is going to fall on top of the hero, her skirt is going to fly over her head and of course his hands are going to land you know where.

Don't make every bit of dialogue, every bit of action a lead-in to a sex scene. When readers finish the book, they should feel that these two people have more going for them than just a supernormal sex life. How do they settle arguments outside of bed?

WRITE A NOVEL, NOT A LECTURE

New romance writers often have stars in their eyes, hoping and expecting to receive reviews that say their books "transcend the genre." But, in their attempts to "transcend the genre," beginners quite often produce works that are not novels but rather long lectures on some issue such as AIDS or battered wives or drugs (usually drugs), interspersing information about the issue with sex scenes. The result is a cross between a free government pamphlet and pornography. Whatever it is, it isn't a romance novel, and it doesn't sell.

DON'T WRITE DINOSAURS

When I was first published, it was much easier to sell a romance novel than it is today. All a writer needed then was an angry hero, a feisty, big-busted heroine and a lot of sex.

But the world back then was virginal compared to what it is

today. Twelve years ago you had to have proof of age to buy a photo of a nude woman. Today perfume ads feature nude women in them. Even though the world has changed so much, too often a reader can pick up a romance novel written in 1991 and find very little difference from a romance written in 1975. In far too many instances, the heroes are still mocking, arrogant and sardonic, and the heroines are still so beautiful they drive men wild with lust; the plots are about a heroine who stamps her foot a great deal, a hero who desires the heroine, a villain who must have her and enough sex scenes to fill 85 percent of the pages. The days when such romances were not only published but also sold millions of copies are dead. Today's readers want characters with complex personalities, not simply hormones that put a teenager's to shame. Readers want a plot that has meat.

STAY WITHIN THE CONFINES OF THE GENRE

When new writers want desperately to sell, they often try to write a "different" romance. This usually means they plan to write a romance with a hero who is a voodoo priest and rather frequently bites the heads off chickens. I've had letters from women who suggest I write a book with a hero who is a wife-beater and reforms. These letters frighten me.

Remember, too, that it's harder to write a good, solid story of love between two people who are rather ordinary than it is to write about characters who are so beautiful that men go insane with lust or so masculine that women kill just to go to bed with them. Such characters simply aren't believable and, therefore, are of less interest to readers.

DON'T PUT ANYTHING INTO YOUR STORY THAT DOESN'T RELATE TO THE STORY

Quite often a new writer will create a long study of the major characters, including physical aspects, personality traits and whatever else they know about the character. Then as each of these characteristics is inserted into the story, the writer marks them off the list. In other words, everything she knows about the character is included in the story. Unfortunately, quite a bit of this information isn't needed and just bores the reader while interrupting the story.

Let me give you an example. Often in the first chapter of a romance, there will be a long paragraph telling the history of the heroine's education. It may state that back on the plantation, her father didn't believe in education for women (this goes back to the ol' persecuted heroine plot), so a tutor was hired for her brother. But the brother was only interested in horses, so the tutor spent his time with the heroine. Because of this, the author informs us, the heroine can read and write two dead languages. After this paragraph the author never again mentions this splendid education, thereby making this bit of information superfluous.

Only information necessary to the story should be included. For example: Say the hero and heroine were tramping about the jungles of South America searching for a lost treasure, and they came upon a stone tablet that had the next clue on it. The hero could brush away the dirt, see that the stone was written in Latin, and say, "Great, now all we have to do is travel six hundred miles back through the jungle to the nearest museum and find someone to translate this." At that time, the heroine could translate the tablet, the hero could ask her how she knows how to read Latin and the author could have the heroine tell the story of her education.

An author should always know more about her characters than she tells the readers. Just because the author knows the hero's favorite food, his favorite color, how he got the scar on his wrist and so on is no reason to bombard the reader with these facts. If there *is* a reason, the story will point it out.

START THE BOOK IN THE MIDDLE OF THE ACTION

Books today must compete with television, movies and video games, so they must be almost as fast and as fascinating.

Stories that start with whole chapters of explanation about the characters are neither fast nor fascinating. When I try to talk to new writers about this, I'm often told that this is "setting the stage" or "developing character." What the writers are really doing is giving away all their secrets at the outset of the book.

Let me illustrate. Say your best friend calls and asks you out to a movie, but she won't tell you what you're going to see. You're game for this so you go to the theater, the lights go down and on the screen comes a man and he begins talking. He tells you all about the heroine's life, about her childhood, about her relationship to her father, that she was upset about her mother's death and on and on. After he gets through with the heroine, he starts telling you about the hero. I think this boring, lecturing man will clear the theater. People today are used to seeing movies in which three people are killed in violent ways in the first four minutes—and that's in a romantic movie.

What if you go to the movie theater, the lights dim. The movie starts and you see a plain with a hill in the background, and as the camera moves closer, you see a single tombstone in front of the hill? Sitting on the tombstone is a young woman reading a book. What the viewer cannot see is that coming toward the woman, over the hill, is a man on horseback riding hell-bent-for-leather, who is being chased by four other men on horseback. Just as the man in front reaches the edge of the hill, he looks down, sees the woman and knows the only thing he can do is try to jump over her. The woman looks up, sees the belly of the horse going over her and falls backward over the tombstone.

This opening, as opposed to the one made up of lectures telling everything the reader hasn't yet wanted to know, asks a lot of questions. What is this woman doing out here alone? Is the man on the lead horse a good guy or a bad guy being chased by a posse? (And my personal question: What in the world is she reading that is so fascinating that she doesn't even hear galloping horses?)

Sometimes a writer will use any excuse to insert her thirty-five or so pages of character study. For example, if the hero and heroine, in order to escape the bad guys, need to hide in a small dark place, and the hero would rather be shot at than climb into this enclosed space, the heroine can later say something to the effect of, "You want to tell me about what happened?" Too often the writer will then have the hero sit down on a log and tell twenty-six pages about his rotten childhood, just as though he's had ten or so years of therapy and can analyze it. It is much more effective to have the hero say, "No." No. That's all. This simple no suggests lots of questions. It makes readers want to find out what caused the hero to be afraid of small places. By doling out the information in small doses, you keep the reader interested and excited.

When you create such questions, you allow readers to discover your characters and live your story as they read it—the hallmarks of all good fiction. And as you create the characters who invite such questions, you'll find you won't need to turn to plots filled with clichés and steamy bedroom scenes.

There are hard-and-fast rules to writing a romance. And the most important is that you must not fail to capture the imagination of readers.

PART 4

Spotlight On . . .

CHAPTER 17

Writing the Short Contemporary Romance

Helen R. Myers

With lives becoming busier and more stress-filled, reading time is more of a luxury than ever. When you add to that the ongoing concerns about paper costs in publishing, it's no wonder the short contemporary romance has gained phenomenal popularity, both in the United States and with foreign markets. Not to be confused with the sweet or traditional romances that run 10,000-15,000 fewer words, short contemporary romances are between 56,000 and 70,000 words and are known as the most sensual of all the series books.

This is where aspiring novelists frequently hone their skills, and I believe it's the best of all training grounds because it is the short contemporary that teaches a writer to be articulate yet concise. My first editor offered the sage advice that "less is more" when you're writing one of these books, and I keep that quote near my computer to this day.

THE BASIC REQUIREMENTS

Writing tight is imperative with the short contemporary because you're expected to deliver gripping, fast-paced stories that are well developed and as thorough as any produced for long contemporary books; however, long contemporaries get an additional 20,000- to 30,000-word leeway. At the same time, short contemporary stories must show particular attention to sensory detail, which is why readers come to the romance novel in the first place. Of course, that attention must complement the type of story you're telling—its premise, the conflict and, most importantly, the characters. For example, a short contemporary drama or mystery will probably be more atmospheric and passionate than a comedy. But not always. Ultimately, it's the voice and vision of the writer that determines the amount of sensory detail in the story.

The "make-it-up-as-you-go" novelist doesn't usually do well in this category, just as a saga writer would have difficulty restraining her expansiveness to the restrictions of a short story. Outlining and keen deliberation are essential if you plan to attempt anything in this format, but don't make the mistake of thinking short contemporaries are formula books. A publisher's guideline is merely your first clue to what works in the series and what doesn't. It doesn't mean you're now safe from making mistakes such as creating a weak beginning, boring your reader with a sagging or unfocused middle and disappointing her with a conclusion that leaves too many unanswered questions and abandoned secondary characters. Do any of those things and you can be assured you won't be added to anyone's must-read list. Assume a reader has only come to you for laughs and titillation, and you've again underestimated category readers. These often well-educated, professional people read widely in other genres and value thought-provoking, broad-scoped stories involving characters who can inspire as well as entertain them.

The writers who learn to be thorough yet discriminating in this shorter length fiction often go on to successful careers in writing more complicated, mainstream books. They've learned the value of framing and constructing their stories well, to choose strong focal points like themes and how to enhance their stories' scopes with powerful metaphors.

In this chapter, I'll explain how I develop my short contemporaries. But remember that just as each book will demand its own tone, each story you write will evolve in its own way. You must remain flexible, and remember to trust your creativity.

ESTABLISHING A PREMISE

A story always begins with an intriguing idea—or does it? Maybe you've been contemplating a trilogy about three sisters, characters that are loosely based on childhood friends. Maybe you've always wondered what happened to them, and you've decided to create an adult life for each. However that first seed for a book comes, whether as idea, character, theme or book title, it's both exciting and a little frightening, isn't it? Something inside you whispers that you have the makings of a good story.

In the case of my RITA-winning book, *Navarrone*, the plot idea came as a result of seeing a gripping story on *60 Minutes* about the indiscriminate and cold-blooded slaughter of wild horses on government-leased grazing land out west, where wildlife has to compete with huge cattle herds for food and water. I couldn't get those images of dead animals out of my mind; nor could I mute my disgust for anyone who could cut down such beautiful creatures for the sake of commerce. I had a hunch that if the idea gripped me, it would also be compelling, and maybe even educational, to readers.

So then, whether you're working from the initial point of idea or characters, the first thing you want to do is establish a *premise* for your story: "This story is about . . ." "These two people are brought together because . . ." No matter what else you plan to do with the story—have your hero and heroine fall in love, conflict rears its ugly head, sexual tension claims its moments—that initial premise must remain as a beacon in your mind, not only affecting everything that happens along the way, but also directing you toward the ultimate destination, which is a satisfying conclusion to the premise and your couple living happily ever after. If someone is murdered, the murderer must be identified and brought to justice. If two people in love have been separated due to some internal or external conflict, that conflict must be resolved in an honest and mature way. The opportunities are limited only by your imagination.

WHO'S TELLING MY STORY?

In the short contemporary romance, the story usually unfolds between two main characters: the hero and heroine. Where once publishers wanted writers to tell the entire story from the heroine's point of view, today we have the freedom to unfold our stories using the viewpoints of both lead characters. Some writers prefer to do this by letting the heroine maintain the viewpoint for one paragraph and then switching over to the hero's perspective in the next.

After writing almost a dozen books this way myself, I realized

I no longer felt comfortable with the style. It didn't feel honest, and it certainly didn't feel focused. So I began to unfold my stories restricting myself to one viewpoint per scene. Does that mean one method is correct and the other incorrect? No. It's a matter of style and preference, the artist's eye. For me, allowing one character to control the whole scene adds power. It also adds mystery and suspense to the action as a result of readers wondering what's going on in the other character's mind. They have to keep reading to find out.

Some editors will allow short contemporary books to include secondary character viewpoints, but this is usually a privilege held for veteran writers. However, maybe you have a unique story that truly requires an additional voice. Don't toss out a wonderful idea simply as a result of this unwritten rule, but do be prepared to compromise and be flexible if the editor asks you to revise. An author's willingness to take editorial direction can be as valuable to a publisher as talent and story.

By and large the hero and heroine in short contemporary romances are very much like the people you meet in everyday life. Like you, they're facing the prospect of the future with excitement and anxiety. They have dreams, goals, strengths and the same weaknesses you do. Gone are the days when the heroine had to be a perfect specimen of femininity, if not physically exquisite, then at least harboring a soul purer than Snow White's. Today our heroines can be plain, as well as pretty; a bit overweight, as well as reed thin; a student or a teacher; unemployed or a corporate executive; single, married, widowed, divorced. The list is almost endless.

In keeping with that change, our heroes are no longer restricted to the alpha male role. He's not just the enigmatic autocrat, the cool, remote scion of some business empire waiting for our sweet and innocent heroine to melt his iceberg heart. Today's hero is a worthy contrast to the exciting and complex heroine. Like her, he has weaknesses; and while he can be an alpha male, since that type of character maintains its share of faithful fans, you should know the vulnerable, sensitive hero has gained admirers, too.

In *Navarrone*, the name for my hero came almost at the same time that I saw the news story about the wild horses. Crazy as this sounds, I'd just learned that Priscilla Presley had given birth to her second child and had named her son Navarrone. Now I am not and never have been a Presley fan, but I was taken with that name and chose it as my hero's.

The name became so predominant in my mind I knew it should be the title of my book as well. What's more, Silhouette was well into its Man of the Month program, and I had a hunch that, depending on how I formatted the story, this might initiate my second appearance in that successful series. That's how Navarrone became the central character of the book. True, my heroine, Dr. Erin Hayes, was a strong, charismatic character in her own right, but Navarrone was more. He was a metaphor for justice. Battered and bruised by the system and those who continued to abuse it for personal gain, he stood as an icon for law and order, willing to risk everything to uphold it.

BUILDING CONFLICT

One of the most difficult aspects of plotting is determining the story's conflict. Too often new writers believe that conflict means squabbling characters. Nothing could be farther from the truth.

Short contemporaries are concerned with internal conflict and external conflict, and while it's perfectly acceptable and desirable to build stories that incorporate external conflicts, a tale about two compatible people who merely have to resolve how to pay the rent in order to live happily ever after promises to be one boring story. But what if you have a couple who were recently married, and the hero has told a major fib about his work so that when he's killed while on a business trip, his bride discovers he wasn't the man she thought she knew. Now, with her ability to trust in shreds and her heart broken, a stranger arrives who says he carries a message from her late husband. There's something about this wounded, mysterious foreigner that's as compelling as he is troubling—until she discovers he *is* her husband! Suddenly you have a story with some depth and challenge to it.

That example comes from my Silhouette Desire *When Gabriel Called*. It's very much a relationship story about two people having to relearn how to communicate and trust before they can attempt to build a marriage that will last. That's their internal conflict. There are external ones, including logistics, such as keeping Gabriel on the premises yet out of Lisa's bed. There's also Lisa's need to deceive people at the school where she teaches, as well as keeping the secret from Gabriel/Jon's old cohorts in the government, who she now knows lied to her. But those externals are secondary to the central and pivotal conflict between these two wounded souls who are still bound by a love they didn't ask for and can't walk away from.

Conflict forces action and reaction in your story. It challenges your characters' goals and affects their motivation. The two-steps-forward-and-one-step-back image works here. Just when you think the couple has made a giant leap of progress, the central conflict reemerges in a unique yet honest way to remind the two of them that there are no easy solutions to life's real problems. If your solutions are easy to resolve, they're not conflicts; they're misunderstandings. And that's not good plotting.

THE LOVE SCENE

Please note that I wrote *love* scene and not *sex* scene. If you can burn that concept, that philosophical nuance, into your mind, you'll have a good grasp of what the short contemporary hero and heroine's relationship is all about. These are monogamous couples with healthy, sexual relationships. There can be flirtations with other individuals but no intimacy. Mores and morals matter to these people, which challenges critics who label these books as soft pornography.

The challenge is to write a love scene that's evocative, not superficially erotic. It's a matter of nuance, of composing a scene where there's psychological union for the characters along with the obvious physical one. As a result, each love scene in a book changes the couple's relationship to some degree. That's why I always tell aspiring writers at workshops that love scenes are a choreographed dance to me. Each move by one character demands some response from the other. Hopefully it's a natural one. There should be a fluid progression in the pacing of the scene that is as seductive as the words we choose to describe what's happening.

Using symbolism and metaphor is an effective and challenging way to continue that process. I'm not talking about euphemisms, although house style will determine what explicit language can and can't be used; I'm talking about continuing the symbolism you initiated in the beginning of your story that represents your hero and heroine. If she is a sunny woman, full of light and life, then the words you choose throughout your loves scenes should complement that personality. Metaphors and similes about light and warmth should appear. If your hero is a dark, brooding personality full of inner turmoil, he should evoke images of such power.

Also remember that a ten-page love scene will be intrusive in an action-packed story. It breaks the momentum as badly as a gratuitous dinner scene added for the sake of word count. Save those longer scenes for stories that are more relationship based. At the same time, remember that not all intimacy means full consummation. Your hero and heroine can create a sizzling moment just from sharing the same glass of wine or canteen of water. Again, you're limited only by your own imagination.

TIPS FOR WRITING THE SHORT CONTEMPORARY

• No one chapter can tell you everything you need to know to write a successful short contemporary romance. The best advice is the same that you heard when you were learning to ride a bike: Practice, practice, practice. But remember that if your first book, and even your second book, is easy to write and sell, chances are the third or fourth—or maybe the tenth—will become the "book from hell" for you. You'll save yourself great pain by remembering and accepting that you're growing with each book (and hopefully challenging yourself with deeper, more skillfully drawn stories).

• Remember, dialogue should be natural. It needn't always be formatted as a complete thought, nor must it always respond to a question just posed. Attributions aren't always needed, especially if there are only two people in the scene. And, no, there is nothing wrong with using the tag *said*.

• There is no rule about chapter length. Just as the story dictates who will best handle the point of view for a particular moment or scene, the destination and goal of the scene will dictate how many pages will be required.

• The mystery and drama in your story will be more compelling if each scene ends with a hook. A provocative question or the shocking appearance of an unexpected character will make it virtually impossible for the reader to put down your novel.

• If you have a prologue, does it mean you'll have to add an epilogue? No. If you find a natural and satisfying conclusion in chapter ten or eleven, then so be it. What's most important is completed logic. Be a thorough thinker, and strive not to leave unanswered questions and holes in your story.

• A romance novel is about feelings. I've found that working like a method actor suits me. If you're feeling the pain, joy and doubt your characters are experiencing, chances are your readers will pick up on those emotions, too. Your goal as writer is to bring two characters through a difficult moment in their lives. They've survived, they've grown as human beings and they're more in love than ever. Any honest person will admit that's really what she yearns for in her own existence, and you'll have shown her an entertaining, tasteful example of how it's achieved.

CHAPTER 18
The Regency Romance

Jo Beverley

THE EVOLUTION OF REGENCY STYLE

On February 5, 1811, the British parliament acknowledged the dismal truth: The king of England, George III, was permanently mad, and his eldest son, the Prince of Wales, must be appointed regent. In effect, Prince George, then forty-nine years old, would act as king until his father died in 1820.

Thus began the English Regency, a period noted for stylish elegance alongside conspicuous excess; for polished manners but also behavior worthy of the most vicious modern gang; for beautiful art and the cruel eye of Rowlandson's caricatures.

In other words, it was a time of contrasts.

Regency style is one of those things we know when we see it. It includes soft-looking, high-waisted dresses and ornate bonnets, gentlemen dressing in well-cut darker cloth and snowy cravats and simple, well-proportioned Georgian houses furnished with gleaming mahogany chairs upholstered in striped satin.

In fiction, too, there is a Regency style. Like the ladies' gowns, it is elegant, charming, often a little frivolous, but built on a very solid structure. Like the ladies and gentlemen themselves, it is regulated by good manners yet spiced with a naughty wit. It is the Regency romance.

THE LEGACY OF GEORGETTE HEYER

How did this Regency style arise? We must look first to Georgette Heyer. This writer of forty historical romances between 1921 and her death in 1975 discovered the special nature of the Regency period and honed and polished its fictional identity. Anyone intending to write Regency romance should read Heyer.

She started writing Georgian books, set in the eighteenth century when aristocratic men and women both wore satin, lace, cosmetics and powdered hair. She could tell these swashbuckling stories well, but high drama and grand gestures weren't really in her nature. She was a stiff-upper-lip English gentlewoman, who, as her biographer notes, "believed in self-control, good manners and form" (*The Private World of Georgette Heyer*, Jane Aiken Hodge).

When Heyer drifted forward into the Regency period, she found her home. Reform, both moral and political, was in the air. Better hygiene and civil administration were creating the modern world. Enough of the Georgian spirit remained, however, to provide material for romantic adventures.

Heyer left a wonderful legacy: a period highlighted for us and a style of books marked by accuracy of fact and tone, peopled by marvelous characters who at the drop of a beaver hat will speak with natural and fluent wit. The characters are her creations, but the period was real, which is why it still fascinates us today.

Some Early Influences

We can distinguish the Georgian and Regency periods in terms of fiction. The Georgian period is *Pamela*, *Clarissa* and *Les Liaisons Dangereuses*. The Regency is Jane Austen's social satire, Sir Walter Scott's historical romances and poets such as Shelley and Byron.

Scott, Shelley and Byron are necessary to balance Austen, for though Austen undoubtedly wrote out of the Regency world, her books do not encompass it. We sell the period short if we forget the drama and high romance of Scott, Shelley et al., never mind the authors of the really popular fiction of the time: the gothic novels satirized by Austen in *Northanger Abbey*. Your Regency heroine might well have read Isabella Kelly's *The Secret* or Regina Maria Roche's *Nocturnal Visit*.

Even the orderly world of Austen suffered the disruption of the men in red coats—the military. The war against Napoleon, with so many young men fighting and dying, brought tension and opportunity.

Take, for example, Arthur Wellesley. A mere younger son, Wellesley was posted to India, "the back of beyond." The military crisis in Europe brought him home and gave him an opportunity to shine. For his military service, he was knighted, then given a viscountcy, then the title Duke of Wellington along with the means to support it. His story was repeated on a smaller scale by many others. Though Regency romances are rarely set within the war zones, it can be an exciting launching pad for a story.

If a dashing military hero doesn't appeal, the war provided excitement at home in the form of espionage, smuggling and invasion threats.

The war also brought wealth to the landowning classes, creating Austen's prosperous gentry and the glittering world of the upper classes within which we so love to play.

REGENCY SOCIETY

War meshed easily with the lifestyle of the typical Regency buck, dominated as it was by bloodthirsty sports, principally pugilism (boxing) and foxhunting. Wellington may not actually have said that the battlefields of Europe were won on the playing fields of Eton (a famous upper-class school), but it was true. Clearly our Regency hero can be any type, but we should not forget that beneath elegant tailoring was generally a very physically fit man.

While Regency men enjoyed pugilism, both as participants and spectators, they were obsessed with foxhunting, particularly in the Shires—Nottinghamshire, Leicestershire, Derbyshire and Rutland, all centered on Melton Mowbray. From early November till March, most men who could afford it were in Melton or the area thinking of nothing but horse, hound and fox. This was no sport for wimps. The injury rate was high, the death rate not insignificant.

These men were matched by as wide a variety of women as we have today. They could be well educated or empty-headed, robust or delicate, active or placid, conventional or rebellious. Thus, the Regency heroine is generally easily understood by the modern reader.

The Regency lifestyle is easy for modern people to relate to.

Gaudy satin garments, panniers, powdered hair and face paint were all passé. Standards of personal hygiene continued to rise, and both police and postal systems were improving, as was transportation.

The London Season

Canals had already revolutionized the transportation of goods, and now toll roads and posting inns made human transportation possible and even pleasant. Thus we have the growth of the London Season—that great Marriage Mart so often the center for a Regency romance.

Before this period, most upper-class families lived in the country year-round. The men visited London because many were members of Parliament. (A peerage title automatically gave membership of the House of Lords, and many seats in the House of Commons were "in the pocket" of aristocratic families and taken by younger sons.) Because travel was slow and hard, however, ladies rarely accompanied their men. In 1785, it could take over three days to travel the 173 miles from Exeter in the West Country to London. By the Regency, it could be done within twenty-four hours.

A social shift occurred, too, beginning in the eighteenth-century Enlightenment. It was now thought desirable for young people to choose their own marriage partners—within reason, of course! This wasn't easy when their suitable acquaintances were limited to the handful of good families within a twenty-mile radius.

For these and other reasons, regional assemblies and the London Season became popular. At the time, they were real centers for intrigue and romance. (In Austen's *Pride and Prejudice*, Elizabeth Bennett is snubbed by Mr. Darcy at an assembly, thus spinning off the tale.) Now, they provide an excellent setting for romance novels since the characters can be trapped in a social whirl, forced to encounter their embarrassments at the next ball or rout.

Or the conflicted hero and heroine could be stuck at a country house party like people trapped in a snowbound cabin. The improved communications made these short house parties possible and popular, but even at the time, they were considered hotbeds of scandal. What more could a novelist want?

The most sparkling and intense gathering, however, was the London Season. Since historically the main reason for going to town was the sitting of Parliament, the Season is related to that; but by this point in time, it had a life of its own. It can be taken to be April to early June in most years.

Presentation at court was an essential part of the Season for women *and men* who wanted to be accepted as part of the *haut ton* (high class), sometimes called the *beau monde* (beautiful world/ people). With the monarchy in such disorder, however, court had lost its power. Ladies would make their curtsy to Queen Charlotte. Gentlemen would make their bow to the Regent. Then both would go play at the balls, soirees and routs of Mayfair.

THE IMPORTANCE OF RESEARCH

Don't even think of writing Regency if you don't like research. Regency readers are avid fans. They not only read many Regencies, they often research the period on their own. Accuracy is a must.

It is easy to gather the basics; after all, the Regency is only a ten-year period. Having grasped the basics, however, we must dig deeper. That's when we find out that the diarists and letter writers of the past left out the things they considered obvious, such as how a young lady addressed a handsome earl, how ladies and gentlemen arranged partners at a dance and what kind of underwear they wore.

Romance has always concerned itself with these matters and still does. Humans live by social rules, especially in the mating dance. In Italy, a man may get away with pinching a woman's bottom to show admiration. Let him try it here! It's become quite the thing for a young woman to ask out the man she fancies. Not long ago she would have been branded brazen or stupid.

So when we are dealing with how a man and woman make contact, navigate courtship and end up joined for life, these little details of propriety, appropriate language and how they get one another out of their clothes can be crucial.

Such social details have become central in the Regency romance for a number of reasons.

First, we have the influence of Heyer, who clearly found manners and mores important, probably because she was raised in a time and circle when complex etiquette ruled.

More importantly, perhaps, the Regency romance is an aristocratic form. Clearly in this period, we have people of all levels, down to the poorest farm laborer or the beggars in the streets. The protagonists of a Regency romance, however, are always of the upper class. The upper levels of any society always have self-generated rules and regulations designed to mark status and to show up those who do not belong. (For this carried to a ridiculous degree, read about the rules of life at Versailles before the Revolution.)

Your characters can move out of the noble setting: Your hero might be a footman or a smuggler; your heroine, a seamstress or a governess. But they will be upper class by birth or breeding, preferably both, and in the end will come to rest in that setting.

Absolute rules for any aspect of creative writing are suspect, but this seems to be the basic criterion of the Regency. Your protagonists can be "slumming it," they can even be vampires or fairies, but they had better fit easily into the aristocratic world. Break that "rule," and even if you have an excellent romance, it probably will not be accepted as a Regency romance by the reader.

These readers choose Regencies because they enjoy the British upper-class setting with all its quirks and follies. Thus it's hard to write a really good Regency unless the writer feels—in her fantasies at least—affection for a society based on good birth, good manners and everyone "knowing one's place."

It's hard to get the upper-class tone right without extensive research, including the correct use of aristocratic titles and a feel in the bones for aristocratic behavior. And the appropriate behavior may surprise someone whose expectations are founded on Victorian, as opposed to Georgian, England.

The Regency still retained much social ease, derived from everyone knowing his place. The rising middle class had not yet made much of a mark. Since Lord Born-to-Rule was confident of his superiority and knew that none of his inferiors would encroach, he was perfectly happy to spend the evening down at the Pig and Whistle downing a jug of ale with his tenants and the local tradesmen.

Social events such as assemblies were not heavily regulated since "everyone who was anyone" knew one another. The only real control was the introduction system. If Mr. Wellbred didn't happen to know Miss Delicious, he could surely find someone in the room who knew both her and him. This person would then introduce him, thereby assuring her that he wasn't an undesirable in a good coat.

If a stranger came into the area, someone would immediately begin one of those inquisitions, "Oh, you must be one of the Derbyshire Wellbreds." Heaven help the impostor who couldn't remember who his great-aunt was supposed to be.

To absorb this subtlety of social organization, read the letters and diaries of the time. Also read plays, which are often even more lively portrayals of the way people interacted.

Social maneuvers are often the very heart of a Regency romance. Though the novels sometimes include crimes, including murder, story lines generally avoid very dark elements in favor of complications arising out of clandestine meetings, scandal or the struggle to enter the right circles.

WRITING THE REGENCY ROMANCE

This chapter has been about what we call the "traditional Regency romance." This loosely follows Heyer's form and is usually a shorter book, between 60,000 and 80,000 words depending on line. Though the political Regency lasted from 1811 to 1820, for fictional purposes, the Regency can stretch back to the turn of the century. It is a courtship book and therefore rarely involves lovemaking within the compass of the novel. This in itself can give a delicious sexual tension harder to achieve in other romances.

Sometimes, if the story involves a marriage, there will be lovemaking, but it will usually be written in a less graphic way than in a historical novel. This, however, is something each writer must decide for herself. Just bear in mind that a reader picks up a Regency expecting a story that reflects the social mores of the times. She will be somewhat disconcerted to find Miss Delicious and Mr. Wellbred out back of the assembly rooms having inventive and spicy sex. (Note that another mark of the Regency romance is the English tendency toward understatement and restraint.)

Since the aforementioned *ton* were generally well read and accustomed to conversing, the ability to talk easily and fluently, and preferably with wit, was highly regarded. This sets the style for Regency romance, where even the most dark and dangerous hero is expected to do more than lean against the wall glowering. When he attacks, it is more likely to be with a cutting tongue than with his fists, though a punishing right is appropriate as a last resort.

Beware, however, of cliché in your portrayal of fashionable life. Yes, the subscription balls held at Almack's on Wednesday nights were important, as was the fashionable parade every day in Hyde Park, but Regency readers are a little tired of the same old round. A great deal more went on, including literary readings, scientific lectures and exhibitions of all kinds.

So in the traditional Regency, we have a distinctive literary form that includes a firm structure and high reader expectations about accuracy. If this does not appeal, it is probably wiser to write in another time and place. If it does, the form itself can be enriching, like the form of the sonnet or haiku.

To Market We Go

Publishing houses: Regency publishers change from time to time. Such information will always be available and up to date in RWA's *Romance Writers Report*.

Money: Traditional Regencies have a solid following, but it is not large, so it is rare for such books to become best-sellers. In 1995, an author can expect (very approximately) a two- to four-thousand-dollar advance and five to ten thousand dollars when all the money rolls in many years down the road.

Prospects: If this is what you want to write, don't let financial details discourage you. No area of fiction, even in romance, promises instant wealth. If you can build a name in Regency and write a number of books a year, you can do quite nicely, and many of the top romance writers today started in short books, including Regency.

The Regency Historical

In recent years, the Regency has become a popular setting for historical romances. The historical reader has no fixed expectations, so the period can be used in any way the writer sees fit. The glittering life of the upper class still has its appeal and is usually used; after all, nearly all British-set historicals have protagonists drawn from the upper classes. Plots, however, can be much darker. Since a historical romance will be closer to 120,000 words, the story line can be more complex, and more elements from other parts of society can be introduced.

Though as a form the Regency historical is more open than the traditional Regency, the requirements for accuracy are as strict, and reading both wide and deep is recommended.

All publishers of historical romance are interested in Regency settings. As for money, at the lower end they will bring an author about the same as a traditional Regency. At the top, we have books on major best-seller lists.

SUGGESTED READING

Erickson, Carolly. *Our Tempestuous Day*. New York: Morrow Publishing, 1986.

Priestley, J.B. *The Prince of Pleasure and His Regency, 1811-20*. Harper and Row, 1969.

The Quizzing Glass, publication of the Beau Monde, the Regency Special Interest Chapter of RWA. For more information, contact RWA. Membership of this chapter will open the door to all the information about writing the Regency you could want.

The Regency Plume, bimonthly newsletter. Annual subscription $12, $16 in Canada, 711 D Street NW, Ardmore, Oklahoma 73401.

Sichel, Marion. *Costume Reference*. Vol. 5, *The Regency*. Boston: Plays, 1978.

Watkins, Susan. *Jane Austen's Town and Country Style*. New York: Rizzoli, 1990.

CHAPTER 19

Paranormal Romance: Time Travel, Vampires and Everything Beyond

Diana Gabaldon, Ph.D.

L et's start by defining a paranormal romance. *Paranormal* is any romance in which either the setting or one or more of the protagonists is "different." He (it's normally, though not invariably, the hero who gets to be different) might be a vampire, for instance. Or he might be an alien. Or a werewolf. Or a citizen of a future civilization. Or a time traveler. You know, *different*.

The one thing that is of inviolable importance in any paranormal romance is that it is still a romance no matter what the trimmings. In other words, you have two people who meet and fall in love, overcoming various obstacles along their path to union.

TELLING GOOD STORIES

There are elements that are common to good stories in general, for example, conflict, characterization and consistency (and a few other items not starting with *C* but important anyway), and to romance novels in particular: A man and a woman who fall in love and, eventually, live happily ever after.

Point 1: A good story is a good story, whether it involves Jane Doe and Joe Blow or the werewolf next door. Paranormal elements alone do not a good story make, and the elements of what *do* make up a good story are largely independent of genre or subgenre (see sidebar on page 150).

Point 2: Genre or subgenre is determined by the inclusion of specific elements. In the case of romance novels, the essential element is the development of a male/female relationship. A paranormal romance is defined by the presence of any element that goes beyond the boundaries of normally accepted notions of reality.

The elements that cause a story to be classified as paranormal may be integral to the story itself or used only as a small gimmick in the plot; however, it is not the use of any of these elements that makes a story either good or salable.

Romance conferences commonly present workshops at which editors from various publishing houses patiently explain what it is they are looking for, i.e., good, fresh, interesting stories. Invariably, an aspiring writer sticks up a hand and begins, "I have a hero who was in a terrible accident, and now he's got like bionic body parts, and is that OK for your line?"

How would the editor know? It might be a great story ("Here was a man who had made the ultimate sacrifice for love. . . .") but the hero's vital statistics, intriguing as they are, simply wouldn't tell you whether it's going to be a decent story or not.

There are principles to good storytelling, and these must not be ignored or violated, just because your heroine is a mermaid.

That said, though, paranormal elements certainly can provide that most elusive of all elements in a romance: freshness. How many ways are there for people to fall in love? Well, maybe half a dozen, if you count forced marriages and marriages of convenience separately.

But say A and B fall in love, and what's keeping them apart is the minor consideration that she's mortal and he's not. You instantly have a more original cause of conflict than the fact that she's feisty and he's an arrogant fathead (aka alpha male).

Point 3: Paranormal elements may or may not be integral to a story but can add to the interest and novelty of an otherwise fairly standard story. Such elements are most effective if the paranormal element deeply affects the characters (see sidebar).

People love romance novels, and the theme underlying all romances (love conquers all) is sufficiently powerful to have motivated most forms of artistic endeavor for several centuries.

Still, one of the reasons for the enduring appeal of romantic stories is that a good romance embodies this ageless theme in the novelty of individuals. It's been four hundred years since Romeo kissed Juliet, but every time two people fall in love, the world is born anew.

The challenge, for an author dealing with such a dependable and ageless theme, is to create new and compelling individuals and to discover the evolution of their unique version of this endless story. In many ways, the use of paranormal elements can help, either in the creation of new and wonderful characters or in the creation of unique and exciting settings and conflicts.

Point 4: Paranormal elements offer the opportunity for literary experimentation and entertainment beyond just the basic romantic story line.

Many literary critics tend to dismiss genre fiction on the grounds that it's formulaic; there isn't anything truly original happening in terms of story or writing, and the conventional elements of whatever genre it is render the book predictable. This certainly can be true, but it doesn't need to be. What literary critics overlook is the fact that genre conventions can be used as a crutch or as a springboard. Louis L'Amour wrote conventional westerns. Larry McMurty writes westerns, too, but I haven't seen anyone dismissing *Lonesome Dove* or *Buffalo Girls* as genre fiction lately.

The use of paranormal elements allows an author unusual opportunities for comedy (time travelers running into archaic customs or modern contrivances are always good for a laugh), for social commentary and for simple escape.

Inclusion of paranormal situations or characters enhances the fantastic aspects of the book. Romantic fiction can include everything from the very realistic to the totally fantastic, but most standard romance novels are in essence fantasy. Paranormal elements can add to the reader's pleasurable illusion of stepping into a completely different world—so long as the first two points I noted above are observed: it must be a good story, and it must still be a romance.

Now to nuts and bolts: What makes a good paranormal romance, and how do you write one?

RESEARCH AND DETAILS

You must provide enough detail to familiarize your readers with the world of the story and make them feel immersed in it. Research is the heart of a convincing historical novel, but the reason *why* this is so applies equally to building a convincing novel with paranormal elements. That is, in order to make the reader enter fully into your story, she must be able to see, feel, hear and otherwise sense where she is.

In a contemporary novel, you need relatively few detailed descriptions to achieve this. You say, "Ted wore a business suit," and you need only add that it was herringbone with a crimson red tie. Bingo! There's Ted. Everybody can see him fine.

Say "Lord Rodrigo flicked a speck of tobacco ash from his jabot and hiked up his hose," and you've got a ways to go. What exactly are hose? Maybe socks, but how much of Lord Rodrigo do they cover? What's he wearing in between the hose and the jabot? Is the jabot that thing around his neck? Meanwhile, the story has moved on, and the reader is still struggling with the not altogether displeasing picture of Lord Rodrigo wearing socks, a lace necktie and nothing else.

The point is that whenever you use settings or characters that are unfamiliar to your readers, you must provide more detail than you do when using familiar ones. Ergo, when you are using time travel, you use precisely the same techniques as you do when writing straight historical fiction; you have to bring another time to life.

Similarly, when you introduce the concepts of alternative lifestyles, you need to provide details as to the Standard Operating Procedures of vampires, werewolves, angels or what have you in order for your readers to enter fully into the spirit of the occasion.

WORLDBUILDING

Writers of novels involving outright fantasy, alternate universe or futurist settings refer to this process of providing detail as "worldbuilding." The process is precisely the same whether you're using a completely imaginary setting, a known historical one or some combinations thereof. The difference is that when you deal with a real historical setting, you derive most of your detail from outside sources; whereas in a totally imaginary world, you may invent more detail.

One point to be emphasized here is that it is *not* necessarily easier to invent details than it is to look them up. Don't believe me? Read on.

Paranormal stories can be set anywhere, any time. However, wherever and whenever they are, the world of the story must be logical and consistent.

This means that if your story takes place on a spaceship, you had better mention the artificial-gravity generator or deal with the effects of sex in zero gravity, but your characters had better not be able to bounce off the walls when making whoopee, then get dressed and walk down the corridor—unless you note that they've turned on their personal antigravity packs at the door.

In other words, you can indeed invent worlds and situations to suit yourself, but you'll have to deal with the consequences. If you've announced somewhere that your heroine time-travels when she looks in a magic mirror, you cannot let her do it by snapping her fingers and whistling "Dixie" backward. If time travel makes her invisible, she'd better durn well *stay* invisible and not pop into sight during the king's dinner party just because you think that would be cute.

Likewise, if you're dealing with situations that are based on natural laws and scientific principles—space travel, planetary colonization, etc.—you can't suspend the natural laws of physics and biology without some really good explanations.

In other words, making things up does not excuse you from the obligation to make sense.

GENERAL RESEARCH TIPS

Now, how to do research? One good way to start is with children's books. These provide a quick, easy read that summarizes the main points of a subject in an interesting way and thus orients you in an unfamiliar field and provides directions for further and more specialized research.

Along the same lines, it's normally better to go from the general to the specific: Learn the major personalities and general time line of the French Revolution before you start worrying about what sort of underwear the heroine should have.

One of the things that leads writers to whine about "all that reeeeeseeearch" is the notion—ingrained by years of school—that you have to *read* everything in all those enormous, dusty books, and then *remember* it all.

Look. Nobody is going to test you on this stuff. All you want is a sense of familiarity with your times or setting and a notion of where to look when you need specific detail. When you pick up a research book, look at the Table of Contents, maybe skim through the Index. That will give you a good idea of what sort of information is in this book. Look at the parts you think might be interesting. Why wade through chapters on the financial policies of Louis XV unless your hero is the Chancellor of the Exchequer?

If you think a book is boring, toss it. Don't waste your time reading boring stuff that will still be boring if you put it in *your* book.

Beyond the library, for those with computers and modems, the online world offers an unparalleled resource for quick, easy and fascinating research. Need to know when fly-fishing was first used? How big an exit wound a .357 magnum bullet makes? How long to wait before you pull the rip cord of your parachute? What kind of underwear Marie Antoinette wore? The Mohawk word for lacrosse?

One or two questions, posted in the right places, can produce detailed answers to almost any esoteric question, often within twenty-four hours. CompuServe's Writers Forum, as an example, has a "Research and Craft of Writing" section, where this sort of questioning is common.

One brief final note on research: If you are dealing with an actual historical period, it's useful to read actual documents of that period—letters, diaries, newspapers, whatever you can find. These will not only give you the best picture of the concerns and cultural attitudes of the times, but will also help you develop a convincing "voice," using the style and idiom of the time.

HOW PARANORMAL ROMANCE IS SOLD

It's perfectly true that paranormal romance is hot stuff these days in terms of marketing. Angel books sell like hotcakes, time-travel stories are at least as popular (if not more so) as straight historical romances and vampires ooze their pallid eroticism from every shelf.

Still, there are pitfalls to writing a paranormal romance when it comes to selling the thing.

The main difficulty in selling a book with paranormal elements lies in the balance of elements. That is, often an author will become fascinated with the details of the paranormal world, or the ramifications of the situation and lose track of the main romantic conflict between the major characters. But most readers of romance are looking for—not surprisingly—romances. They will be displeased if the hero and heroine stop experiencing sexual tension for long stretches in order to deal with minor things like political assassination or interplanetary bank robbery. Ergo, refer back to point 2; it still has to be primarily a romance, or you will have difficulty in selling it as one.

THE ELEMENTS OF STORYTELLING

I should point out that this list is my personal opinion, and not the official rules that everyone is so worried about breaking. The three main elements of a good story:

1. Character
2. Conflict
3. Consistency

All good stories stem primarily from good characters. We must have at least *sympathy* for the main characters, if not actual identification with them. Consequently, characters must be recognizably human, even if they have a few small idiosyncrasies, such as drinking blood and baying at the moon.

The story must be based on a believable conflict. This may be external (circumstances like wars, plots, epidemics and general persecution affecting the characters), internal (factors of individual psychology and background that make it difficult for a character to achieve her goals) or both. The heroine taking exception to the way the hero looks at her is not a believable conflict.

Consistency means (1) that you may not violate the rules of your own universe, whether that universe is the normal one or an invented one, and (2) that you likewise may not violate the integrity of your characters. A heroine painted as intelligent and competent should not lose her head and behave like a pea brain only because *you* can't think of any other way out of a situation.

THE STEPS OF A GOOD STORY:

1. Introduction of character/setup of conflict. These happen as soon, and as interestingly, as possible.

2. Action. Things need to be happening as soon as possible; there's always time for talk later.

3. Character. This is key. Things happen in a story because the characters are who they are. If you understand this, you will not have any particular problems with plots.

4. Resolution of conflict. The conflict(s) introduced at the beginning of the story must be resolved by the end.

CHAPTER 20

Elements of Romantic Suspense

Eileen Dreyer, aka Kathleen Korbel

J.P. is a man on the run. An undercover cop who has unearthed dangerous information, he's been arrested for the murder of his partner. What J.P. has ended up in, besides jail, is a suspense novel. From this point, he can look forward to a big dose of danger, mystery and action.

But J.P. doesn't stay in a suspense novel. He makes a decision that completely changes his status. In a desperate attempt to escape and clear himself, he kidnaps his beautiful defense attorney and holds her hostage.

ROMANCE—WITH A WHOLE NEW SET OF RULES

What J.P. has just done is not just dangerous, not just insane. What J.P. has done is change the book he's in from a suspense to a romantic suspense. From this moment on, the mystery of who set up J.P., the chase J.P. finds himself in to rescue important evidence before he's caught, the danger he faces in avoiding capture and death all involve a woman—a woman J.P. will inevitably fall in love with. And because of this, J.P. will find himself not only shelved in a different section of the bookstore, but bound by an entirely different set of rules for getting out of his predicament.

The bad news is his problem has become more complicated.

The good news is that it's also become a lot more fun.

J.P.'s new world of romantic suspense is a hybrid, an entirely unique genre that is the result of the careful grafting of romance and suspense parents to create a stronger, more unique whole. Each of the parent genres is easily identified in the resulting product, but because of the way the two are joined, their offspring ends up with a completely unique identity.

If I were to name the focus of each parent genre, I would say that romance is to characterization what suspense is to plotting. There have been wonderful romances that have been weak on plot, and great suspenses in which the characters were no more than cardboard cutouts. After all, we didn't watch *Raiders of the Lost Ark* so we could find out what made Indiana Jones so restless. We wanted to see how he was going to rescue Marian. We didn't even care that he had a father until Sean Connery was needed to set off the action in *Indiana Jones and the Last Crusade*.

In romantic suspense, you get two for the price of one. Both character and plot play an equal part in making a page-turner.

SOME NOTEWORTHY EXAMPLES

The best romantic suspenses are easy enough to recognize. Any list of favorite movies will inevitably contain at least a few romantic suspenses. *Charade, North by Northwest, The Big Easy, Witness*—just the titles alone evoke images of a man, a woman, a puzzle, terrible danger and, yes, raging hormones.

Like any good romance, those movies wouldn't have made a dime if they hadn't given us wonderful chemistry between the hero and heroine. Like any good mystery, they wouldn't have been satisfying if the danger hadn't been very real, the mystery very puzzling, the outcome satisfying and logical. And, like a good story of any kind, if these characters hadn't been compelling, no audience would have cared enough to see if they lasted through whatever peril they were put in.

For instance, we've seen movies before in which a cop is chased by the murderers he suspects of a bad crime. We wouldn't have *Witness*, though, if the cop weren't a hardened, driven, upright cop caught in a strange land with a compassionate, strong Amish woman. On the other hand, we wouldn't have had a romantic conflict if that cop hadn't been thrown together with the woman because her son witnessed the crime the cop is trying to solve. Characters and plot, plot and characters neatly entwined to make a satisfying whole (although, admittedly, the classic romantic suspense ends up happier for the hero and heroine).

Would *The Big Easy* have been worth sitting through twenty times if Dennis Quaid hadn't had that alligator and Ellen Barkin that button-down suit? Would their relationship have progressed as it did without the New Orleans city corruption? Would the stakes have been so high without their attraction and his possible complicity in murder?

So, like a good recipe, you begin with simple ingredients.

THE ESSENTIAL INGREDIENTS

In romantic suspense, you start with two compelling characters who are about to fall in love completely against their wills while trying to solve a puzzle that will save themselves and possibly the world as they know it from grievous harm. Simple. The real talent lies not just in the ingredients used, but the manner of mixing.

A Relationship

Obviously, if romance is involved, there must be a relationship. The difference in romantic suspense is that the relationship between the hero and heroine must have to do with the suspense. If, for instance, we are writing J.P.'s book, in which he finds himself on the run, he can't fall in love with the local schoolteacher unless she's the one he kidnaps or the person who helps him solve his mystery. Luckily for him, he falls in love with his defense attorney, Lauren.

Likewise, in *Witness*, there would have been no earthly reason for Harrison Ford to develop a relationship with Kelly McGillis unless her son had witnessed a murder. Dennis Quaid and Ellen Barkin wouldn't have developed that particular relationship in *The Big Easy* unless she were investigating him.

It is possible to hide or mislead the audience as to the reason the relationship is integral to the suspense. For instance, for quite a while in *The Big Easy*, neither the audience nor Dennis Quaid knows that Ellen Barkin is investigating him.

There is also the thrill of the unknown. One of the favorite devices in romantic suspense is the "Is he or isn't he?" theme. Who exactly was Cary Grant in *Charade*? Is J.P. really the hero to the lawyer, or is he lying through his teeth just to get free? If one character keeps coming up with knowledge he shouldn't or behaving in a way that doesn't seem logical, the stakes are raised nicely.

The rule here is, of course, that the other character must react logically to the possible threat or subterfuge (if a heroine really believes a guy might be a murderer, she wouldn't go off into the woods with him simply because she was feeling passionate). Also, in the end, the subterfuge must be not only explained but explained to the audience's satisfaction.

The growth of the relationship between the hero and heroine must mirror the growth of the suspense. As in any good plot, each scene must build on the one before, increasing the tension both in the romance and the suspense as the book progresses. The ante has to build relentlessly.

In *Witness* again, Harrison Ford has two face-offs with bad guys. The first time, he's simply doing his job. He's angry and righteous. By the second time, though, the stakes have changed. He has fallen in love with the woman he's protecting. She has given him back his humanity. He fights for her, for the child, the family and the world she cherishes and has taught him to love.

In the case of J.P., because she begins to fall in love with him, the lawyer he's kidnapped deliberately moves from captive to active role in helping him. By the end of the book, both she and J.P. risk their lives, their reputations, even their sanity for each other.

The relationship must not only impact the decisions made in the suspense, but the events in the suspense must impact the relationship. In *The Big Easy*, Ellen Barkin loses her objectivity about her suspect (Dennis Quaid) because she's falling in love with him. But when Dennis Quaid ruins evidence to protect himself from prosecution, she loses faith in him and leaves. Because he's falling in love, he works hard enough to win her back that she ends up including him in the murder investigation she's conducting. Because of her impact on his life, he changes his behavior as a policeman and investigates his own police family. Back and forth, the impact of a decision from relationship to suspense and back again provides the warp and weave in the pattern of the romantic suspense.

The wonderful thing about combining the action this way is that you have the luxury of geometrically increasing the level of tension in the book because you're doing it on two fronts at once.

Sexual Tension

Let's address the important issue of tension in romantic suspense. Sexual tension is almost always heightened in a romantic suspense because danger is the greatest aphrodisiac. It's a variation on the old war theme, "But honey, we could be dead tomorrow." Few things set off a relationship faster than being in a terrifying situation. Adrenaline makes all the glands work better, so it shouldn't be a surprise that the ones responsible for reproduction should demand equal (if not more than equal) time. Especially if a good-looking man is the one saving our heroine from the bad guys.

Emotions are heightened, tensions need to be relieved, and with two people who are falling in love, it's no surprise they end up in a similar position to the one Dennis Quaid and Ellen Barkin occupy so imaginatively in *The Big Easy*.

Not only does the impact of characterization intensify your suspense, but the elements of the suspense add depth and conflict to your characters. The best conflicts in a romance are the internal conflicts. But more often than not, internal conflicts are brought to light by external conflicts. If Harrison Ford had not been shot by the bad guys in *Witness*, he might never have realized what he was missing in his life. If J.P. had never kidnapped Lauren, he never would have admitted how lost he was. Lauren would have never assessed the impact her childhood had on the rest of her life.

So the book must have the emotional impact of a romance. But it must have the plot of a suspense.

A Logical Plot

The plot must be logical. This means that there must be sufficient motivation to see the plot through, both in the relationship and the mystery. We would no more want to solve the murder halfway through the book than the relationship.

The characters must be well-enough drawn that each of their decisions makes sense within the context of the action and their characters. Try not to rely on contrivances simply to further a plot. How many people have spent a good portion of a horror movie yelling, "Don't go down the stairs"? You don't want your audience yelling that at you. Every action must have a reason, and a darned good one. If the lawyer decides to trust J.P., there has to be something in his actions that would convince any woman that he is more than a fugitive desperate enough to do anything.

The ends must justify the means. As Chekhov said, "If there's a pistol hanging on the wall in the first act, it must be used by the third." And vice versa: If a pistol is used in the third act, it had better darn well be on the wall in the first. The seeds of the solution must be planted all the way through the book. On the other hand, they can't be too obvious, at least to the hero and heroine, or the audience will lose respect for them if they haven't figured the thing out by chapter four.

The romance should complement the suspense but never interfere with it. The hero and heroine can get into more trouble because they can't keep their hands off each other (in *The Big Easy* Ellen Barkin gets involved with Dennis Quaid even though he's a conspiracy suspect), but they cannot take a four-hour break in the middle of a desperate chase to make love simply because there aren't enough sex scenes in a book.

The rules of logic are relentless in a suspense. If you're not sure whether a romantic encounter is disrupting the action, picture fifty police stamping their feet in the snow and looking at their watches while waiting to start the chase again as the hero and heroine roll around in a barn fifty feet away, screaming in ecstasy.

The action must move, figuratively and literally. These are action books, home of the simple declarative sentence. They entail car chases, gunfights, things that go bump in the night. A suspense is not the hero and heroine talking for thirty pages about what's happened. Stick them both right in the action, and then let them figure a way out. If a body is discovered, the heroine should be the one to do it. If there's a gun-toting crazy person, the hero should take him out, not the local cop who just happens to show up.

The hero and heroine have to be integral to the solution of the suspense. Unless one of them has a badge, it should not be the police who solve the mystery. After all, it isn't the police's story.

That said, the solution of the suspense must also provoke the solution of the relationship. When our heroine Lauren survives the incredible ride with J.P., she realizes that she's been too afraid for too long to take a chance, and she knows J.P. offers her freedom. J.P. realizes he's been given another chance to redeem himself with Lauren, and they end up together. In *The Big Easy*, Dennis Quaid ends up facing off with his own brother police to solve the homicides, thereby discovering an honor he never thought he had and becoming worthy of Ellen Barkin's love. The murders solved, they finish the movie dancing in wedding attire.

Appropriate Use of Language

One final thing I'll throw in regards the use of language in romantic suspense. The language of a suspense book is traditionally more spare and "clean" than romance. Romance books are far more sensuous, imagistic, poetic. The language is emotion driven and the descriptions immediate and intimate. Most of the good romantic suspense books, like those written by Nora Roberts or Tami Hoag, employ language that is more reminiscent of romance than suspense. Even so, because of the action involved, the results are a mix.

A balance should be struck: a bit leaner than a character-driven romance, but more intimate than the average suspense novel. Remember, not only are you killing people, you're making people fall in love. And while murder scenes usually demand simple declarative sentences, love scenes do not. The best way to understand this is just to read good romantic suspense and pay attention to the words.

There are some excellent authors to recommend for study. Besides Nora and Tami, I would also recommend, among others, Paula Detmer Riggs, Jayne Ann Krentz, Anne Maxwell, Patty Gardner Evans. Pick your favorites. Then pick their books apart to find out how they do it so well.

Oh, and J.P.? He showed up in a Silhouette Intimate Moments I did entitled *Walk on the Wild Side*. It ended up being a pretty typical romantic suspense with, as I've said, a mystery, car chases, gunfights, love scenes, a little angst, a little more humor and a lot of action. It's my favorite kind of book. After all, as I've always said, if you're afraid of your romance becoming too boring, put a bullet through the window and see what happens. I mean, I haven't seen *The Big Easy* twenty times because I like the Neville Brothers.

CHAPTER 21

The Medieval Maiden

Susan Wiggs

W hat fictional character sings like a golden harp, speaks three languages, rides like the wind, weaves masterpiece tapestries, wields sword and longbow like a warrior, settles legal disputes, raises babies, organic produce, and animals, practices healing arts and feeds a household of hundreds on a daily basis?

If you answered "the medieval maiden," you're right.

THE UNIQUE APPEAL OF THE MEDIEVAL ROMANCE

One of the reasons for the enduring popularity of historical romances set in medieval times is that readers and writers alike have a special affinity for this character. In any given month, new releases from publishers are bound to include books with medieval settings. Editors are always looking for a new and exciting tale of Welsh mysticism, Highland raiding, Norman conquesting, Viking invasion or a good, solid English-castle-under-siege yarn. Each of these stories must feature colorful pageantry, feats of derring-do and, of course, a passionate love affair between a knight in shining armor and a damsel who will knock him silly if he dares to suggest she is in some sort of distress. Sure, she has her share of troubles, but she's not about to step back and let the hero sweep them all under the rushes.

A medieval romance is like others in the genre in that it must be a compelling story of a great love that ends in triumph and happily ever after. However, there are some aspects that are unique to the medieval romance.

Often, it's the story of a quest or a great battle. It might be a captor/captive romance, a secret baby or an arranged marriage story line. Themes of personal family honor often take center stage in a medieval. Power struggles between factions or families are often a metaphor for the battle between forces of good and evil, light and dark.

These are "classic" story lines—*not* formulas. The writer's task is to bring the story to life in a fresh and unique way. The key to setting your medieval apart from all the others is to create a riveting, one-of-a-kind cast of central characters.

Regardless of the author's choice of plot and theme, a medieval romance is *always* the story of a fascinating woman facing a tumultuous conflict.

THE "LARGER THAN LIFE" HEROINE

So what is she like, our medieval maiden?

First of all, she's not necessarily a maiden. She might be a widow, a prostitute, the victim of rape, a happily (or unhappily) married lady. Virginity (or the lack of it) is very likely to play a part in your story, but there's no rule that says our heroine has to be virginal. The important thing for an author to do is to make her a believable product of her time as well as a compelling character for the reader.

Although the ladies in contemporary tales of courtly love and in Victorian constructs were often depicted as delicate blossoms, these characters are figments of the (usually male) poet's or painter's imagination. Real women of medieval times had to be strong and sturdy as noble oaks. Failure to work hard and to develop survival skills often had dire consequences: starvation or invasion, robbery or rapine.

Daily life in medieval times tended to be demanding physically, mentally and emotionally. Our medieval maiden rose with the dawn, worshipped at regular hours throughout the day and was responsible for any number of chores, from inventorying the contents of the buttery to collecting rents to raising children.

The medieval heroine must function in a society that had only recently emerged from complete barbarism. Her world was balanced precariously between the primitive and the civilized. While barbarians might be pounding at the gate, in the scriptorium a scholar might be composing an epic poem. At any moment, the picaresque world contained within the town walls or castle gates could be burned to ashes or pounded to dust. This gives medieval plotlines a dramatic sweep and a compelling edge that readers find hard to resist.

Tapestries, frescoes and paintings often depict the medieval maiden as a dainty lady doing needlework in her solar. It's pretty to look at but not very realistic. The woman as decorative ornament was the fantasy of wealthy men who wanted to show the world that they were so rich their women didn't have to work.

Romance readers and writers know that women have always worked. Peasant and urban women toiled as the poor always have. In the medieval town and countryside, women labored as farmers, brewers, merchants, weavers, servants, prostitutes and manufacturers. A noblewoman running a castle keep had to master a staggering array of skills, including administrative, bookkeeping and accounting chores, healing, gardening and many other domestic skills. Christine de Pisan was a noted author, Eleanor de Montfort kept exhaustive control of a vast household in peril, Eleanor of Acquitaine had the sharpest political mind of her age and Boadicea fearlessly faced the legions of Rome.

In wartime, the lord of the keep was often absent. He might have been away on crusade, serving the king elsewhere, doing a stint in Parliament or traveling his remote lands. For the romance writer, this presents a tempting menu of possibilities. During the lord's absence, the chatelaine might be called upon to defend the estate. This means she'll need some grounding in military matters, she'll need to know how to give orders and she'll need to understand the rudiments of weaponry and warfare.

Or perhaps, in the absence of her husband or father, she meets an intriguing stranger. And perhaps this stranger has some sort of grudge against the lord. The possibilities are enticing. A fact of medieval life suddenly becomes a springboard for fiction.

In the medieval romance, there is often a conflict between society's misogynistic view of woman, man's passion for control and the reality of a woman's considerable strengths and abilities. In her heart, our medieval maiden is likely to be fiercely independent. She'll resist a man's attempts to dominate or subjugate her. She will give her all to protect what is hers. That's one of the things that makes her so much fun to write about.

The more you read and learn about women in the Middle Ages, the more you'll wonder where all those paintings of limp-wristed, sighing maidens came from. In my reading, I've discovered that most medieval maidens were bright, competent and courageous. The ones who weren't simply didn't have the right stuff to survive for long.

In *Medieval Women: A Social History of Women in England, 450-1500*, by Henrietta Leyser, the research goes far beyond the stereotypical damsels in distress, redeemed fallen women or snow-white virgins. We meet women who manage their own property and their own lives. Who could resist Annabel, the cow-keeper who fractured a thief's skull defending her cattle? Or Adela, daughter of William the Conqueror, whose bedchamber featured a mosaic map, tapestries with historical scenes and a detailed painting of the zodiac.

The medieval maiden was quite likely to be both literate and numerate. Bequests of books as well as scholarly and scientific materials were quite common. Our heroine was not, alas, permitted to serve in a civic office, but she might have been a member of a guild, a smallholder or the proprietor of a small business. A villainous sort—or maybe even the hero—could challenge her in a lawsuit, or she could challenge him.

Yet, despite her many skills, the medieval maiden was still expected to ride pillion behind the man in a man's world.

Most texts and treatises on the "proper" upbringing of girls instruct them to be sober and dutiful, biddable, pliant and pious. One quote from my reading really struck me: "Subdue the passions and press them down." (St. Jerome)

How many of us have ever felt forced to subdue our passions? *Press them down* is a powerful image. It implies an almost physical level of self-restraint.

When I read this, I had to ask myself why. I could only conclude something that's perhaps as true today as it was five hundred years ago: Society as a whole is afraid of a woman who lives a passionate life and gives free rein to her emotions and desires. Whenever possible, society tries to subjugate a woman's passions, including her intellectual life.

Those in authority (in medieval times, this meant men and the

Church) were horrified by those things a woman could do and a man couldn't, such as menstruate. According to author Frances Gies, menstrual fluid was known beyond a shadow of a doubt to cause new wine to sour, crops to become barren, grafts to die, seeds to dry up, fruit to fall off the trees, steel to become dull. It drove dogs mad and infected their bites with incurable poison. During the moon's eclipse, sex with a menstruating woman brought disease and death.

So not only do we cause rabies, but I suppose you could use us for insecticide, too!

The point is, that attitude is pervasive. Women are scary creatures. So it's best to press them down and restrain their passion.

THE READER'S FANTASY

One of the aspects readers seem to find so gratifying in a medieval is the fact that, in the resolution of the love story, the hero is made to accept that the woman he loves is a strong, brave, independent person, not his inferior. Throughout the book, he has been testing her, pushing her, trying his best to press her down. Time and time again, she has confronted his aggression, his suspicion, his insistence on mastery. And since this is romance fiction, she makes a believer out of him at last. It won't be easy for her—nothing worth having is easy—but in the end, she gets her way, and he gets the woman of his dreams—the woman he didn't even realize he wanted until he found her. We love to read scenes in which our hero tells her, "Don't change. I love you the way you are."

That's the fantasy. When set against the backdrop of the Middle Ages, it takes on the patina of a fairy tale.

The medieval maiden (though in the resolution she is a maiden no more!) learns and grows throughout the course of the story as well. She finds a way to be her passionate, independent self within the constraints of society and within her love relationship with the hero.

Readers love to see a woman rising to the challenge of a difficult or seemingly impossible situation. Her actions, of course, often rouse consternation, disapproval or even anger in the males around her. Throughout the course of the story, the hero is likely to become exasperated—but never to the point of outright violence against the woman. A hero worthy of the name doesn't need to resort to violence, and an equally worthy heroine would never stand for it. The push-pull of the hero and heroine or the heroine and society can be richly dramatic, creating conflict and even humor.

Writers should work hard to make the heroine as interesting as the hero. Don't write a character who waits around for a man to enter her life before she even *has* a life. She should have a past, a goal of her own and a confidante, often a handmaid or confessor or older companion. Give your heroine the same high stakes in the plot the hero has. Give your reader a character to sympathize with, agonize with and cheer for.

To make sure you've created a woman who is both larger than life and a believable product of her time, do copious research. I cannot stress this enough. Research is the key to bringing your story to life. Sometimes it's the key to your story. Period.

While browsing through a history of the Battle of Agincourt, I was caught by the life-or-death struggle of King Henry V's march through Normandy. The men of his army were sick and starving, yet he had to cross a river and do battle with a French army that was four times larger than his. The plot of my medieval romance, *The Lily and the Leopard*, sprang almost full-blown into my head at that point. King Henry's need to cross the river Somme set off a chain reaction of what-ifs in my head. What if a certain castle happened to be situated at the perfect spot to ford the river? And what if a lone woman, loyal to the French, commanded the castle? What would the king do?

Order his most trusted knight to marry the woman and take control of her château, of course!

I had a lot more work to do on that plot, but the seed of the story grew out of a very narrow, specific historical incident. Keep your eyes and ears open for these gems. You never know when the magic will happen.

Not long ago, my young daughter spied a yellow hummingbird buzzing past our front porch. Without hesitation, she said, "Look! A fairy! We have a fairy in our yard!" And I felt highly privileged to live in a house with someone who believes so absolutely in the existence of fairies.

Such is the appeal of the medieval maiden heroine. She has an unshakable faith, a powerful belief in the supernatural as well as a sense of knowing her world and her place in it. Her life is not simple and neither is she, but she moves within a solid framework that is attractive to modern readers.

In *A Natural History of Love*, by Diane Ackerman, the author describes medieval storytellers and songsters known as the troubadours. This will sound uncannily familiar to a dedicated romance writer:

> What fascinated the troubadours were the first stages of love, whose flickering emotions they chronicled, the trembling moments at the beginning of an affair when two lovers were transfixed by one another, absorbed into each other's version of reality, but quivering with uncertainty. . . . They preferred the lying awake at night, the devoured glances, the secret codes, the fetishes and tokens, the steamy fantasizing, the moaning to one's pillow, the fear of discovery, the agony of separation, the torrents of bliss followed by desperate hours.

What better job could we want? We *are* the troubadours!

SUGGESTED READING

Romances that feature memorable medieval maidens:

Alinor and *Rosalynde*, by Roberta Gellis

A Bed of Spices, by Barbara Samuel

Bride of the Lion, by Elizabeth Stuart

Candle in the Window, by Christina Dodd

Dark Champion, by Jo Beverley

Falcon's Fire by Patricia Ryan

Here Be Dragons, by Sharon Kay Penman

In Pursuit of the Green Lion and *A Vision of Light*, by Judith Merkle Riley

Katherine, by Anya Seton

Knight Dreams, by Suzanne Barclay

Lion of Ireland, by Morgan Llywelyn

For further reading:

Anglo-Saxon England, by Frank Stenton

The Anglo-Saxon Home and *A History of Domestic Institutions and Customs*, by John Thrupp

Anglo-Saxon Women and the Church, by Stephanie Hollis

A Baronial Household of the Thirteenth Century, by Margaret Labarge

The Beginnings of English Society, by Dorothy Whitelock

Daily Living in the Twelfth Century, by Urban Tigner Holmes, Jr.

Death and Life in the Tenth Century, by Eleanor Duckett

The Decameron, by Giovanni Bocaccio

A Distant Mirror, by Barbara Tuchman

Growing Up in Medieval London and *The Ties That Bound*, by Barbara A. Hanawalt

Growing Up in the Thirteenth Century, by Alfred Duggan

A History of Their Own (Vol. 1), by Bonnie S. Anderson and Judith P. Zinsser

The Knight, the Lady, and the Priest, by George Duby

The Letters of Abelard and Heloise, by Betty Radice, trans.

Life and Work in Medieval Europe, *Medieval Nunneries*, *Medieval People* and *Medieval Woman*, by Eileen Poser

Living in the Tenth Century, by Heinrich Fichtenau

Marriage and the Family in the Middle Ages and *Woman in the Middle Ages*, by Frances Gies

Medieval Culture and *Medieval Households*, by David Herlihy

A Medieval Home Companion, by Tania Bayard

Medieval Idea of Marriage, by Chris Brooke

The Medieval Woman, by Edith Ennen

Medieval Women: A Social History of Women in England 450-1500, by Henrietta Leyser

A Natural History of Love, by Diane Ackerman

A Political and Social History of Tenth and Eleventh Century England, by Pauline Stafford

Standards of Living in the Later Middle Ages, by Christopher Dyer

Women in the Medieval Town, by Erika Vitz

Women's Lives in Medieval Europe, by Emilie Amt, ed.

CHAPTER 22

Writing the Historical—Then and Now

Jennifer Blake

The Flame and the Flower was the beginning. With the publication of this book in 1972, Kathleen Woodiwiss established historical romance as a viable form of genre fiction. The stories as conceived by Woodiwiss were linear descendants of such classic romances as *Jane Eyre* and *Gone With the Wind*. In keeping with these books, plots were complicated and concentration was on a female protagonist and her goals. The love affair between heroine and hero was the central issue and, as such, was portrayed as a grand and timeless passion. This male-female relationship was placed in its proper perspective as the single most important alliance in existence, the driving force behind the perpetuation of the human species. Titles for the books in the early years, such as *Love, Forever More*, *The Storm and the Splendor* and *Love's Tender Fury*, celebrated this aspect.

The genre also owed a debt to mainstream historical romance novels of the 1940s and 1950s, books that were themselves derived from the chansons de geste of the troubadours. As with the male protagonists of these earlier stories, genre historical romances sent heroines on quests for love and adventure during which every possible impediment was placed in their way. By so doing, they tapped into the adventuring spirit that lies dormant in most women, bringing it out to be explored in the fantasy world of this new literature.

Elements of the gothic novel were included as well, particularly the use of atmosphere to heighten the emotional intensity of the story, the trick of casting the male protagonist as both hero and villain and the requirement that the heroine save herself at the climax of the story.

Add the ambiance of the sensual classic *Forever Amber* and you have a formidable mix.

The greatest innovation, however, was that these stories dealt with sexual intimacy from the female's point of view rather than the male's. The love scenes were never about, as one writer phrased it, "who puts what where" but were an exploration of the heroine's reactions. Written with all the sensual detail implied by that choice, they were less about the goal of sexual completion than about the process of reaching it and its ultimate meaning. This approach made them perfect vehicles for delineating character, since human beings are never more true to themselves, never more emotionally exposed than in the act of love.

Yet, within this component was an even more important detail. As a final touch of genius, Woodiwiss included the sensual fantasy of forced sexual intimacy. With this much-debated addition, the stories gained a male-female conflict with true emotional complexity. It upped the ante of the story, creating the most serious impediment to the prospect of a happy ending for the boy meets girl story ever to appear in fiction. By it, the wronged heroine immediately gained the moral high ground. Though the hero ordinarily committed his crime against her through error, he was still forced to recognize his failing, to repent of it and atone for it. The manner in which this emotional issue was resolved dictated the success of the novel. And with it, historical romances acted as a subtle metaphor for the past injuries of all women, as well as suggesting the eventual means of redressing them.

There was also an essential theme in this story line, which was that there is no "fate worse than death." The implicit assumption was that this is a male concept grounded in the historical supposition that women are chattels whose value can be destroyed by unauthorized sexual congress. To refute it, the bedding of the heroine was treated as a simple assault that, while painful and emotionally wrenching, failed to devastate her. The fact that she could wring some pleasure from the act was her triumph; she did not participate in her loss of innocence so much as gain ascendancy over it.

There were other factors to this scenario. It removed the ancient "burden of consent" from the heroine, allowing her to accept her sensual awakening while placing responsibility squarely on the hero's shoulders. It permitted readers to identify with a heroine so desirable, so intelligent and so independent that the hero was tortured by his inability to possess her mind and spirit as well as her body. Finally, it allowed the heroine to prevail since she not only defeated her enemies, but conquered the man who had dared take her without consent. A vital component of the ending was the hero's impassioned declaration of love and devotion, which signaled his surrender.

Early in the game, Rosemary Rogers introduced *Sweet, Savage Love*, a historical romance with a slightly different twist. The Rogers heroine endured a variety of violent encounters with different men, yet survived magnificently to defeat those who had harmed her and win the hero. As a result of this alternate scenario, there soon emerged two distinct forms of what came to be known as "bodice rippers" (due to the heroine's clothing being reduced to tatters during her struggles). The first, based on the Woodiwiss prototype, concentrated on the emotional relationship template. The second placed the emphasis on the daring quest of an adventurous woman.

Regardless of the exact format, the new genre represented a potent fantasy, one that struck a responsive chord in the newly emerging woman of the sexual and feminist revolutions. Millions validated its innate appeal by snatching copies off the shelves. In response, the publishing world exploded with variations and imitations. "Captive" books, with the hero as pirate or brigand, feudal lord, sheik or prince, flooded into the marketplace.

The backlash began almost immediately.

The books cut too close to the bone for many. Critics deplored the sex and violence, were made uncomfortable by the celebration of feminine sexual pleasure. Unable to distinguish between natural sensuality and pornography, they dismissed the entire genre with the charge of "soft porn."

Feminists were particularly incensed by what they saw as the subjugation theme, railing against it loud and clear. They failed to see or appreciate the inner strength of the heroine, concentrating instead on her apparent passivity and the supposed degradation of her sexual initiation. The much-repeated protest became, "Rape is a crime of violence!" Any plea of extenuating circumstances was rejected with the assertion that a sexual penetration to which the woman had not given her enthusiastic verbal consent was automatically a brutal act of domination devoid of passion.

Due in part to the combined outcry, the use of forcible seduction began to die away. Another important cause, however, was the natural progression of the sexual revolution: Women were becoming more aggressive about their needs and desires so were less likely to feel that a heroine who cooperated in her loss of virginity was a fallen woman. But the main cause for the demise was that it had been used so often it turned into a cliché.

It was at this point that the top echelon of historical romance writers began searching for different male-female conflicts that would still retain the required sexual tension and emotional impact. The arranged marriage became a favorite. Also useful was the exchange of the heroine's favors in return for life-saving intervention by the hero, intimate revenge, the compelling effects of some potent aphrodisiac, the death-threatening isolation of the couple and so on. Some of the furor began to die down.

The practice of having the hero indicate his intense passion by tearing the clothes from the heroine also declined. Sheer repetition had made it an ineffective device; after the first years, the majority of historical romance writers refrained from so much as a torn ruffle. By then it was too late. The term *bodice ripper* was so catchy and had become so universally recognized that it remained in place.

However, there was a problem. With the loss of the power behind the forced intimacy scenario, sales declined. Editors and agents began to look around for something to replace the risk quotient, to "turn up the heat." They demanded more and more detailed, sexual content:

"Spin it out. Give us love scenes that last for seven (nine, eleven) pages."

"Include four (six, eight) love scenes. The reader should be able to take a book off the rack and find something hot anywhere she opens it."

"Variety, give us variety! Let them do it on the stairs, in the carriage, on horseback—anywhere except a bed!"

In time this trend died away, too, done in by the indignation or guffaws of the authors—and the sighs of exasperation from readers as they skipped over the gratuitous coupling. Sensuality in historical romances leveled off to a norm dictated by the characters, the plot and the emotional intensity of the individual book.

Regardless, the need for variety of some kind to sustain reader interest remained. A portion of the slack was taken up by deviations in time periods and locales. As Medieval and southern settings waned, Victorian and western tales waxed. Viking and pirate heroes gave way to outlaws and Indians. Masked and mystery heroes on the order of the Scarlet Pimpernel or Robin Hood made their appearance and became a mainstay. Then, about this time, another major change occurred.

From the time of its inception, popular fiction was written primarily in third person, using the internal viewpoint of the protagonist. In historical romance, this was the heroine, and all aspects of the relationship between her and the hero were filtered through her sensibilities. Many titles of the genre's middle period, such as *Vixen in Velvet*, *Gypsy Lady*, *Adora* and *A Lady Bought With Rifles*, reflected her central importance. Then, with the publication of *Shanna*, Woodiwiss introduced the viewpoint of the hero. This addition, without expanding into full omniscience, was a stylistic departure considered unacceptable by the writing establishment. Nevertheless, it worked in historical romance.

The hero had always been recognized as a keystone; he was required to be a superior specimen of manhood in order to fulfill the expectations of the heroine and the reader. With the new access to his viewpoint, he gained extra stature. The main reason was because it was impossible to create an internal dialogue for him without turning him into a more interesting and complex character.

Then as time passed, authors began to tinker with his essential persona. The powerful, dominating hero dubbed the "alpha male" was set aside for one deemed more politically correct, the helpful, tender and friendly "beta male." When it was discovered that this character type lacked the forcefulness required to satisfy the fantasy, he was exchanged again for something between the two extremes.

Heroines also underwent a metamorphosis, partially in reaction to changes in the hero, but also in response to social and market shifts. The traditional female of breathtaking beauty, intelligence and daring was set aside. In her place paraded cute and spunky heroines, authoritative heroines, vindictive heroines, lame, scarred, myopic, plump, skinny, clumsy, tall and short heroines—whatever the imagination could produce. Role reversal became popular, with the heroine dressed up as the pirate or highwayman. She was often the character scarred and tormented by the past and forced to overcome the resulting mistakes and negative character traits in order to find love and happiness. Sometimes she rescued the hero in a physical sense, while it was he who defeated her demons. She was no longer necessarily young, a circumstance that reflected the aging of the basic reader base made up of women from their mid-thirties to mid-sixties. Because it was unlikely an attractive female over twenty would be inexperienced, the heroine was portrayed on occasion as a betrayed woman, a widow or even a femme fatale.

Emotional content for the books varied as well. The dark-toned, passionate intensity between hero and heroine was often replaced by bright, humorous interaction; warm, secure, home-and-hearth type attachment; or a fey, legendary relationship.

Sequels, the interconnected stories of the lives and loves of one dynamic family similar to the family sagas of the 1950s and 1960s rose as a trend. Later, supernatural and fantasy aspects crept in, with lovers as ghosts, fairies, vampires and so on. Time travel became popular since it allowed a successful juxtaposition of the modern, liberated woman against a hidebound, authoritative male.

So an endless parade of diversity was tested in the marketplace and either approved or discarded. This market testing has never stopped. It still takes place on a daily basis as each new book appears on the shelves.

What, then, makes a historical romance novel today different from the books in the beginning?

One of the main changes is in the length. Originally the books weighed in at an average of 150,000 words, with 200,000 not uncommon. Few top 125,000 now, while many have 100,000 or less. Increases in publishing costs account for the difference, but the result is less space for description of settings or for exploring motivation and character. There is also less allowance for scenes to build the emotional attachment between the two main characters.

Plot structure has been dramatically changed by the shorter length as well. In general, the complex plots of the past based on the fortunes of war or the intricacies of political machination have given way to stories driven by the needs of the two main characters. It is the manners and mores of any given time period, rather than historical events, that have the most profound effect on the key players.

Still the adage that the more things change, the more they remain the same holds true for historical romance as for all else. As greater numbers of authors have entered the field, they have conscientiously bent their efforts to making the stories work, so they have revised and refined the essential features that caused success in the first place. The authors who reach the best-seller lists seem to work with similar constructs, taking the best from the past and adding their own original twists for contemporary consumption. They have distilled the basic historical romance into a mythical fable of good vs. evil in which the heroine braves great danger to conquer the dark forces in man-the-hero, with the essential shift in power between the two being brought about by love.

Perhaps the most striking difference in historical romance today, however, is the steadily increasing importance of the hero. He has come to dominate the books to the point that many now glorify his role by carrying titles such as *Prince of Midnight*, *Chieftain* and *Lord of Hawksfell Island*. The most extreme example of this trend is the elevation of cover model Fabio to the status of "author" and hero of his own tales with titles like *Pirate* and *Rogue*.

In the nonfiction anthology *Dangerous Men and Adventurous Women*, Jayne Ann Krentz asserts that readers actually identify so strongly with the hero now that the female protagonist has become a mere place holder, her only purpose being to establish the reader's connection to him. The contention is that female readers are rejecting the less active role of the heroine for participation in the problem-solving aspect of the male protagonist. While this may be a factor in the increased interest, it does not fully explain it.

Women in society at large are consolidating the gains made by the feminist movement while trying to mend the rift between the sexes caused by the battles of the past decades. In reading romances, they don't identify with the hero so much as empathize with him; they don't want to be him, but rather to understand his thought processes, his hopes and fears. This empathetic understanding is then carried over to the men in their lives.

As romance novels have matured over the past decades, their role as a means of communication between men and women has become clear. Women often read pertinent passages to their partners or mark them to be read. Mental health practitioners and marriage therapists routinely suggest that dysfunctional couple read them for the insights to be gained into the male-female dynamic. The books are recommended as affirmations of the freedom of women to explore their sensuality. Most of all, with the social changes of recent years, their ability to validate the magic of spiritual bonding between a couple within a committed monogamous relationship has become a powerful consideration.

All of which is not to say that romance authors deliberately set out to compose primers for successful interaction between the sexes, or even that individual writers are aware of that possibility as they create their fictional love affairs. It is, in the main, an unconscious process brought about by the natures of the writers, their subject and their audience. Yet, it seems safe to say that as the genre continues to evolve, the synergy between the author and reader, between where women are in their lives and where romance novels can take them will only strengthen and improve. It should be fascinating to see where it will lead in the future.

CHAPTER 23

Writing the Young Adult Romance

Sherry Garland

Writing for young adults is not for the faint of heart. Of all the fiction genres, the YA category is one of the most unpredictable. Like the characters in the stories and the adolescents who read them, YA novels bridge the space between childhood and adulthood, and that bridge is very shaky.

The YA category embraces many subgenres—mystery, horror, romance, mainstream, historical, fantasy and science fiction. YA romances range from fast-paced paperback series to hardback mainstream literature. The difference between these extremes is the market for which each is aimed. Paperbacks are marketed through bookstores, grocery stores, book clubs or school book fairs. Girls buy these books for themselves with their own money. Rarely does a girl plop down fifteen dollars for a hardback YA novel.

Hardback YA novels, on the other hand, are marketed through schools and libraries. Librarians stock few paperbacks, since they fall apart too fast. More often than not, the hardback YA romance is not labeled as such, even if it has a strong love line. Many of these hardbacks are later released in paper and make it into the retail market.

THE BIRTH OF A NEW GENRE

The YA genre is a recent phenomenon. A few series for girls—*Nancy Drew, Trixie Belton, Sue Barton, Cherry Ames*—flourished during the

1950s. However, YA literature did not blossom into an established genre until the tumultuous 1960s, which brought a wave of realism. Authors portrayed teenagers as troubled, tortured beings, struggling to become adults. The "problem novel" covered every topic—drugs, teen pregnancy, incest, alcoholism, runaways, gangs, delinquents, war. Librarians and teachers welcomed this new breed of literature aimed at restless junior high and high school students.

The late 1970s and 1980s saw the "golden age" of YA romance series, and many new publishing lines sprang up to accommodate the voracious reading appetite of girls aged eleven to thirteen. Lines such as *Sweet Valley High*, *Sweet Dreams*, *Cheerleaders*, *Wildfire*, *First Love*, *Seniors*, *Sisters* and *Crosswinds* dominated the paperback market. Between 1981 and 1985, the *Sweet Dreams* series alone sold almost nineteen million books. These books had predictable plots and were "squeaky clean"—no sex scenes, no profanity, no sad endings. Topics centered around friendships, cheerleading, being popular and dating. Typical settings included the mall, the prom, the skating rink, sports events, the high school. The protagonists usually attended middle-class schools.

By the early 1990s, the popularity of YA romance series was plummeting. Horror series took over the role as king of the paperback market. Several YA romance lines folded, and YA romance authors turned elsewhere to make a living.

CHANGING TRENDS

Today, YA romance is making a comeback in a new guise.

First, many publishers are aiming their romance series at a younger audience: middle-grade girls aged eight to twelve. These books often feature "clubs" with several female characters. The protagonists in these books attend junior high school rather than high school or college. These series often revolve around a mutual activity, such as horseback riding, skating, ballet, or baby-sitting. Romance in middle-grade novels means a boy-girl relationship without sex, and often it means first love.

For older readers, realistic contemporary YA romances are gaining in popularity. The protagonists are in high school or college and face the problems of life, love and sex in the 1990s. Typically, the point of view shifts among several primary characters, including the males. Often these appear as a "miniseries" of three to five books written by the same author. These books are more sensual than the "sweet" series romances of the past, and the characters face tough issues.

A few packaged series such as *Sweet Valley High* and *Sweet Valley University* remain popular. The plot is fast paced, the romance is the focus of the story and the setting is the school, the classroom and outside activities, such as sports events, concerts and the beach.

Another trend is to combine romance with elements of other genres—like horror, mystery, fantasy or history. History, by the way, does not necessarily mean something long ago and far away. To teenagers, the Vietnam War era is history.

As for hardback YA romances, although the market is small, the need for quality YA literature has never diminished. These romances contain elements of the mainstream novel and focus more on the problems of the heroine than her love interest. Themes often pertain to social issues or the heroine's coming-of-age.

TODAY'S READING AUDIENCE

Because of television, movies and news headlines, today's young readers are exposed to sex, violence and the darker side of human nature. They mature faster and date sooner. Remember the 1950s when girls didn't date until they turned "sweet sixteen"? In contrast, today's girls are dating (and having babies!) in junior high. Young romance readers fall into three age groups: 8-12 (middle grade), 9-13 (young YA) and 12 and up (older YA). By high school, most teens are either reading adult books or not reading at all, except for English class assignments.

Also because of television, today's readers are highly visual. They are used to things happening instantly with the flip of a switch. They have less patience for long, boring stretches of description. They want to be plunged into the action immediately, and they throw themselves, heart and soul, into the story. They *become* the protagonist, and they may even imitate her. For that reason, your heroine should be a strong, courageous and admirable role model.

Today's readers come from many different cultures. YA novels should reflect the cultural diversity of schools, especially if the setting is a large city. This includes not only students, but teachers and administrators as well. Stereotyping, however, is not acceptable, and cultural accuracy is crucial.

Young readers want to read about characters older than themselves. If you are writing for girls aged nine to thirteen, the heroine should be at least fourteen. The hero should be the same age or a year or two older than the heroine. In junior high or high school, just one grade level can make a difference in peer approval. However, having a mature man court a teenage girl is a no-no.

TABOOS STILL EXIST

While the topics of today's YA romances are more mature than in the past, taboos still exist. *Romance* does not mean explicit sex. Here is an example of a YA love scene from my mainstream novel, *Song of the Buffalo Boy*, aimed at ages twelve and up. Loi, a seventeen-year-old Amerasian living in Vietnam loves Khai, a tender of water buffaloes, but her family arranges for her to marry an officer in the communist government. Loi and Khai meet at a romantic jungle pool, and she gives him the news. Khai feels depressed and defeated until Loi asks him if he recalls their pledge of love three years before:

> "Yes, I remember every word we whispered. And I plucked a white orchid and put it in your hair." Khai gently brushed her hair back from her cheek. His fingers felt rough from the harvest work, but they were warm and tender. Loi's heart beat faster as she looked into his large, dark eyes. She longed to hold him close and feel his heart pounding next to hers, imagining the sound would be loud and strong, like thunder. She reached up and cupped her hand over his, drawing it closer to her face. Closing her eyes, she breathed in the dusty odor of his fingers.
>
> "Tell me, Khai," she whispered, "was it just the idle promise children so often make and soon forget?"
>
> Khai lifted her hand to his nose, inhaling deeply.
>
> "No, beloved. It was not a child's promise. . . .
>
> As much as Loi desired to clasp him in her arms, she dared not move any closer. Other workers were coming for water, and she had stayed too long already. She quickly filled the water jug, and they parted.

That was the big "love scene" for the novel. Loi does nothing more than hold hands with Khai, yet the readers know they love each other deeply and will risk their lives to be together.

Here's an example of a love scene aimed at younger girls, ages eleven to thirteen, from *Opposite's Attract*, a Bantam *Sweet Dreams*, by Linda Joy Singleton.

> David put his hands on my shoulders and answered by pressing his lips lightly against mine. It lasted only a fraction of a second, but I liked how it felt. And when he pulled away—perhaps from embarrassment—I leaned toward him and offered my lips again.
>
> The offer was accepted and this kiss lingered. . . . I had never felt happier in my whole life.

Far more important than graphic sex scenes are the underlying emotions of the boy-girl relationship—the jubilant joy of being together, the excruciating pain of separation, the insecurity, the fear, the conflict and tension and the triumph of that first love.

As for profanity, while some of the mainstream novels include cursing, the YA series romance does not. If the plot requires profanity, whether from shock or anger, use description rather than speech. For example, "he spewed out a string of curse words that shriveled my toes," gets the point across without having to use profanity.

YA romances usually require happy or at least hopeful endings. In either case, the protagonists should grow; they should learn something from the experience that has transpired for the past 40,000 to 65,000 words. They learn about themselves, about love and relations, about life. When finishing a YA novel, the reader should put it down not with the feeling of "the end," but rather with the feeling of "the beginning."

HOOKING YOUR READER

When writing YA romance novels, here are some pointers to keep in mind:

1. Open with a hook—action, a problem, a change. Today's teens are used to television, videos and movies and want to get into the story immediately.

2. End each chapter with a "catch" or "cliff-hanger" to make the reader want to continue.

3. Make dialogue believable, but avoid contemporary slang that will probably be out of date by the time your book is published. Avoid profanity.

4. Avoid excessive description; teens don't have the patience for it. Fast-paced novels have lots of dialogue. Replace adjectives and adverbs with strong, descriptive verbs.

5. Avoid lengthy flashbacks that slow the action. Reveal background material in dialogue and short flashbacks.

6. Use sensory perception—the five senses.

7. Don't preach. Moral lessons should be subtle and shown rather than told.

8. Let the protagonists solve their own problems rather than having an adult do it for them.

9. Do not include explicit sex scenes.

10. To develop conflict and tension, give the protagonist other problems and interests besides the romance.

The market for YA romances continues to fluctuate and requires diligent market research. The author of YA romances, perhaps more than other genres, must keep abreast of the changing market trends. This means reading a lot of current YA romance novels, studying publisher's guidelines, and keeping an eye out for new publishing projects. Although writing romances for young adults is challenging and frustrating, one thing is for sure: Girls will always be interested in boys.

CHAPTER 24

Long Contemporary— Indians Without Cowboys

Kathleen Eagle

The title assigned to this chapter is a thought-provoking one, certainly for me. The first time I saw my Lakota (Sioux) husband, he was dressed like a cowboy. He worked on a cattle ranch, participated in an amateur rodeo and dreamed of becoming a rancher himself one day. He was also enrolled in a federally recognized tribe, lived on a reservation, was educated for the most part in "Indian schools," "danced Indian" at powwows—in short, knew exactly what it meant to be a cowboy *and* what it meant to be an Indian in the twentieth century. And I will say right up front that if you want to write fiction about either, good resources are in short supply. The working cowboy is a dying breed, and the twentieth-century Indian (unless he owns or operates a casino) is largely ignored.

INDIAN VS. NATIVE AMERICAN

Let me digress for a moment and address the political correctness issue. Most Indian people that I know still use the term Indian when speaking of the indigenous people of North and South America. Anyone who was born in America is native American. The size of the *N* isn't much of a distinction. Non-Indian people have been known to check the *Native American* box on everything from surveys to census forms. To be absolutely correct, use the name of the tribe or band. These are truly nations of people, but we've lumped them together in our thinking and in our teaching. In the Dakotas, if you're sojourning in Indian Country, everyone who isn't Indian is non-Indian. Yes, you do hear *white*, but the term *anglo* is not commonly used there. Bottom line: If you intend to write about a real tribe (a word that is also not universally applicable), do your homework. You cannot assume that what's true on the reservation in your area is true everywhere.

When I started writing contemporary series romance, there was a subgenre of Indian romances, but they were primarily historicals. Generally, they were white captive fantasies—I've heard them referred to as "pirates in buckskins"—and they are just as popular now as they were in the early 1980s. Very early on, I decided that my own writer's vision did not lend itself to that kind of book. A writer's most important tools include her vision and voice, and vision is shaped by experience. When I started writing commercial fiction, I had been living on an Indian reservation, teaching in one of those Indian schools, and I was living with an Indian husband and our three children. That's my experience. I've been asked what background I had that qualified me to write about "the Indian experience," and that's it. I'm a mother, a neighbor, a wife, a family member. I'm also a first-hand observer. But I am still non-Indian. I don't write about the Indian experience so much as I write about the experience of a non-Indian sojourning in the Indian world.

One of the primary viewpoint characters in my books is always non-Indian, usually female. That's me. For the most part, that's my reader. That character is a touchstone for writer and reader, and my book becomes a bridge between the world I grew up in and the world that adopted me as an adult. No, I don't claim to be an "adopted member of the Sioux tribe." That's one of the Hollywood-isms I'll get to later. It was once suggested to me that rather than move to the Dakotas to teach (and marry my husband) maybe what I was meant to do was teach "my own people" what I knew about Indian people. At that point it wasn't much, and at the time, I wasn't interested. But what I've learned is that in order to get to know Indian people we have to be willing to learn *from them.* I'm writing primarily to entertain, but the entertainment industry has done

Indian people an enormous disservice over the course of the last century by perpetuating stereotypes. A good writer understands the difference between stereotype and good characterization, knows where good characters come from (flesh and blood, not film) and builds them to be believable as people.

But we want to write about Indians because there's a market for these stories. And there *were* white captives, weren't there? Indeed, there were. The captured bride can make a wonderful story. The skilled writer can make any premise work by playing to the universal qualities that make us all human while building characters as memorable individuals. Just remember that the "noble savage" is a stereotype. I've been asked what was wrong with the "noble savage." It's kind of a tribute, isn't it? No. It's an over-simplification, and it's condescending.

AVOIDING STEREOTYPES

Good guy or bad guy is not the point. A stereotype has only one dimension. When a writer throws in a stereotype, she says, "You know this guy. He is what he always is, just what you expect, just the way you like him." It's lazy writing, and it's generally forgettable because the character blends into the tradition of its type. I think Indian stereotypes persist because Indian Country is little known and much misunderstood in most of America. We non-Indians presume too much; we're more willing to talk than we are to listen, and we believe in the stereotypes *we* have created because we've steeped ourselves in them.

Old-style westerns are riddled with stereotypes. I grew up with television and movie westerns—*loved* them—and so did my husband. But guess what? The whooping "savages" that poured out of the hills on the silver screen scared him when he was a child as much as they did me. He rooted for the guys in the white hats, just as I did. There was seldom an Indian viewpoint in those movies, and if there was, it came from white historians and anthropologists speaking for Indian people. Until quite recently, there were rarely any Indian consultants involved in filming anything about Indian people. Movies and television seldom make good sources for the writer, but we have to remember that they are ingrained in our subconscious. We have to educate ourselves about the people who live and breathe. Good fiction takes the reader beyond stereotypes and introduces her to characters who talk like, act like, think like, feel like real people.

When a non-Indian writer, like me, has the audacity to portray an American Indian as a viewpoint character, she has to somehow make it her business to find out as much as she can about what it's like to live inside the skin of an American Indian. The first thing she has to realize is that most of what has been written and almost all of what has been filmed about American Indians has been and continues to be produced by white men. Not that this material can't be useful—our home library is well stocked with it—but I do urge you to evaluate it carefully. Always consider the source. Consider the writer's background, and remember that every writer's work is shaped by his viewpoint, his experience, his values.

A non-Indian writer who writes about Indian culture, no matter how learned she is, no matter what her sympathies, is still to some degree an outsider. Often her stake in the culture she's writing about is purely academic. The work may be useful, but it doesn't tell you very much about gut-level feelings or faith, and it often misses the mark on motivation. For those of us who write fiction that deals in relationships, insights into feelings and faith are the soul of the story. We've got to get to the heart of the matter. Our character-driven stories thrive on motivation that lives in the blood.

CREATING BELIEVABLE CHARACTERS

How do you get characters to live and breathe? You take the details from life. Not the *events* of life—the events, or at least your characters' involvement in them, are fictitious—but the *way* of life. The way of talking, the way of moving, the way of thinking and feeling and the *sense* of life—the way it tastes and smells and sounds. If you propose to write about Indian Country, where are you going to get the kind of detail that will bring your characters and your setting to life? Books and movies are only a start. Whenever I feel as though I'm getting stale, I know I need to get back to the source, back to the experience, back to the lifeblood—back to the Dakotas. And if you're going to write about Indian people, you're going to need living, breathing sources.

Or you can write fantasy Indians. You can certainly make up a tribe and invent a reservation. I've done that myself because I wanted to deal with an issue without getting into the particular politics of a real reservation in my story. Fantasy Indians are in some ways more palatable in historicals because time adds so much romance to the past. When your characters ring true as people, the reader may well buy into whatever Indian background you create, even if you're basing your fiction on fiction. I don't recommend it, but I don't deny that it can be commercially successful.

Here are some steps you should consider taking before writing about "Indians without Cowboys":

1. Take everything Hollywood ever taught you with a grain of salt, with the exception of some wonderful performances by Indian actors: "Chief" Dan George (the term *Chief* is not native; the white man and the U.S. government invented it) in *The Outlaw Josey Wales* and *Little Big Man*, Graham Greene in almost anything and the supporting cast in *Dances With Wolves*, to name a few.

2. Recognize stereotypes for what they are: flat characters, one- or, maybe, two-dimensional; lazy writing at best, insulting and harmful at the other extreme. Common stereotypes: Bloodthirsty Savage, his sage and stoic brother Noble Savage (often the captor), Tragic Victim, Angry Outcast, Tragicomic Drunken Indian. The whole "vanishing race" image is a myth that relieves us of our responsibilities in the present day. ("What a noble people. Too bad they fell off the edge of the earth.") Notice that there is a kind of half-truth in every stereotype: yes, there are nobility, anger, victimization and alcoholism, but what else? A stereotype is a caricature with no depth and therefore no real humanity. It's a hollow shell.

3. Read American Indian writers. Pay attention to the voice. Personal favorites: Simon Ortiz (poetry and short stories); James Welch; Louise Erdrich's *Love Medicine*; memoirs "as told to" Richard Erdoes, including *Lame Deer, Seeker of Visions* and *Mary Crow Dog, Lakota Woman* and more being published all the time.

4. Bring depth to your research with primary sources. Even if you invent a tribe, you need to know something about federal laws. Tribal law varies from one people to another, as do position titles, treaty status, terms. Your state's attorney's office or congressional representative can help you research federal law, treaty rights and state agreements. Tribal colleges can also be very helpful, as can state historical societies and museum bookstores.

5. Travel. To achieve a sense of place, you must *seek to sense* a place. Talk to people. Indian people are not the humorless stoics they've often been made out to be. They are individuals. There is such a thing as "Indian humor." If you're to write about it, you need to experience it. If this is your life's work, you owe yourself and your work some time spent with the people you're writing about.

6. Remember that values are intrinsic to viewpoint. All too often the nobility of our Indian heroes is grounded in non-Indian values. Indian people do not believe (traditionally) in man's dominion over nature. We tend to look at this as sentimentality and at their faith as superstition. We trivialize what we don't understand. But consider how important this way of thinking would be if your story dealt with, say, mining. To the Hopi, a coal field is the liver of the earth. To the Lakota, the heart of the earth lies in the Black Hills. To Indian people, spiritual practices are a source of knowledge that need not be tested by the scientific method. Much of white America regards tribalism as primitive, something to be liberated from. To Indian people, it is the fabric of community. And the Indian community values the extended family and intergenerational residency (another source of traditional knowledge), while mainstream America values the nuclear family. If your story concerns the adoption of an Indian child, those sometimes conflicting values are going to come into play. The writer must recognize that if she's going to create a viewpoint character who comes from a culture that's different from her own, she can't just plug her own values into her characters.

But the beauty of romance is that love, honor and respect really can build bridges. As people get to know each other and come to love one another, they will find ways to transcend their differences, even to appreciate them. Thankfully, the ability to love, honor and respect is universal. Romance celebrates our willingness to use that ability, and what a great attribute!

CHAPTER 25

Mainstream: It's Not Just a Longer Category

Janet Dailey

WHAT'S THE DIFFERENCE? MAINSTREAM VS. CATEGORY ROMANCE

Category romance is a wonderful thing. I was inspired to write as a direct result of reading category romances, and I wrote sixty-eight of them myself. But category and mainstream romance are two different things. Readers pick up category for a flight of fantasy, a quick escape from the workaday world, a piece of candy for the soul, a burst of stimulation, which is just fine, and, yes, it takes a talent to write and write well. But, aside from the armchair travel necessary for setting, few people think the world of category is anything like the world we live in. With category, readers are not just *willing* to suspend disbelief, they are *eager* to suspend disbelief. It's an expected part of the experience, closing the door on everyday reality for what will hopefully be an exhilarating romp in a "wouldn't it be grand if" sort of pretend world.

Mainstream readers, on the other hand, literally *challenge* an author to make them believe. Mainstream readers are *on the lookout* for unbelievable aspects of a novel. Now, don't get me wrong, we're talking about mainstream *romance*, which means that the readers are looking for an experience they probably wouldn't have in their own lives, an experience that is somehow bigger and more intense than anything they will experience in their own lives. But in order to *have* that experience, in a mainstream kind of way, they have to be able to identify with the characters' emotions, to *feel* with those characters. They won't be able to do that if the plot is false, if the language of the book is false, if the circumstances of the characters lives are false. In other words, every aspect of the novel must ring true if the reader is going to achieve the act of faith—the belief, the identification, the involvement that is the magical act of communion between author and reader that makes for great mainstream fiction.

First, let's consider what mainstream fiction is *about*, or, more specifically, what it's *not* about. The focus of mainstream romance must be more than just a love story. Sure, there's a central love story in every mainstream romance, but whereas the love story can function as the be-all and end-all of category romance, a mainstream novel has to be *about* something larger. For example, in my book *Rivals*, the focus of the story is the rivalry between two powerful families. The love story develops within the context of that subject, according to the dictates of that context. So, while in category romance the plot develops according to the demands of the love story, in mainstream, the situation is reversed, and the love story develops in a natural way out of the elements surrounding it.

That's believable because it simulates reality. No romance exists in a vacuum. The romantic love we enjoy in our lives grows out of the circumstances of our lives—what we do, who we are, where we came from and where we are going—those things influence the courses our love lives take. It should be likewise in mainstream fiction. As another example, in *Masquerade*, I place my protagonist at the center of a mystery, a swindle that threatens to bring down a business empire and also threatens my protagonist's life. The course of the love story within that plot is affected at every turn by the circumstances of the larger story. If I were to reverse the rule and introduce an artificial plot twist, the only purpose of which was to, say, get my lovers into bed together, then I would run the risk of completely destroying my credibility with the reader.

So there are two points to remember about mainstream romance: Number one, if Tarzan spends all his time with Jane and never goes off to fight the bad guys, he's not mainstream anymore, he's category. And, number two, if I cause an elephant stampede for no other reason than to get Jane into bed with Tarzan, I've pretty much destroyed the illusion of reality.

WRITING THE MAINSTREAM ROMANCE

In essence, we want to create a logical series of events within which our characters can function and feel in a consistent way. We don't want things dropping out of the sky. We want our characters to get from point A to point B on their own steam. In order for them to do that, we have to know *who* our characters are. We begin to know who our characters are by establishing *what* they are, something that is part and parcel with what the book is *about*. I'm talking specifically about occupation.

For example, in the book I'm working on now, my protagonist runs her own personal security firm. The book is about the personal security business, which is a growing phenomenon that I got fascinated with and, therefore, provided the germ of concept I used to build the book around. The character's occupation tells us certain things about the character. She started the company, so she possesses a high degree of initiative. The job involves an element of danger, so she must possess a degree of physical courage and so forth.

The point is, everything about a character must contribute to a consistent definition of that character, including his occupation. A clichéd occupation, of the kind often found in category, such as oil man or real estate magnate, does nothing to define the character, unless it's an unusual variation on the theme. In that respect, it's a dead-end street, just like an artificial plot twist. Everything must contribute to the whole.

Beyond occupation, what a character is is defined by more than what he *does*. We all have personal traits that rise from our blood or our souls or some other mysterious sources that have nothing to do with the hats we wear. We are all many-layered, and our characters should be likewise. How do we ferret out those traits for our readers to understand and identify with? One way is through physical descriptions.

It may seem like a paradox to try to know the soul through the flesh, but that's exactly what needs to be done. When describing a face, the point is not the shape of the features so much as their qualities and what those qualities speak about the person. We must try to look at the physical person and see the spirit. On a lighter note, eye color in mainstream should be blue or brown. Amethyst, jade and sapphire should be restricted to jewelry, and keep all fire in the fireplace because eyes need to do something more expressive than burn, blaze or even smolder.

In the same vein, Shakespeare asked, "What's in a name?" and the answer was a resounding "Not much." In mainstream, it's all right for characters to have names like Joan and Ann and Jim and Pete. Colorful names are fun, but strictly forbidden in mainstream. I myself have sinned, even recently. In *Rivals*, I named my main female character Flame, and what do you think the critics chose to rake me over the coals about? The point is, small things like names or the color of eyes can inject a jarring note of artificiality into a book that can go a long way toward shattering the mood of believability you have worked so hard to establish throughout. And all of this relates to language, the style in which you write.

DEVELOPING YOUR OWN STYLE

When I started writing for Harlequin, I threw myself into the fun of it wholeheartedly, and my prose was as purple and as flowery as lilacs in May. And I still have to fight this today. The thing is, I think purple prose is something readers expect from category romance—and actually enjoy. They've picked up the book for a flight of fancy, and fanciful use, or, at times, misuse, of the English language is one device to heighten that mood. But again, the use of bombastic, overheated, overwrought, overworked and overloaded language can destroy the reader's sense of belief, even if every other element of the novel rings true.

Avoid saying things that the average, reasonably sophisticated person couldn't say without a smirk on his face or that might provoke nervous laughter in mixed company. Use the words desire and passion only when they have absolutely nothing to do with either sex or love. Use words like darts, not hand grenades. On the surface, florid, feverish words seem to carry more power, but in reality, they carry less because they lack all subtlety of definition. You'll find you have a great many more tools in your arsenal if you can learn to make ordinary language do extraordinary things. OK, "Me Tarzan, you Jane" is no doubt overly terse, but look at the weight of meaning that laughably simple phrase has come to carry in the public colloquy over the years. Think of "Go ahead, make my day." Simple words from the mouths of strong characters in potent situations can carry ten times more meaning than some of the overworked words we use as crutches or shortcuts to real expression. In category, where the characters are often two-dimensional, it makes sense to speak in two-dimensional language. Fully realized characters, on the other hand, can infuse every dimension of meaning into the most commonplace words.

Peripheral Characters

What about peripheral characters? In mainstream, they should have a real function and real definition, or they shouldn't be there at all. Peripheral characters in mainstream can't be mere conveniences who advance the action and are never heard from again. If you describe characters or give them important pieces of dialogue, they should have a relevance that continues through the novel. I recall in one of my categories, I wrote a scene with the heroine's parents early in the book and never brought them back again. I actually got a letter from a reader complaining that she couldn't help but worry about what had happened to those people.

In fact, peripheral characters, like every other aspect of the novel, should make an important contribution, not just toward advancing the plot, but also toward understanding the motivations of the central characters. You can get a great deal of valuable information from peripheral characters, either directly, through dialogue, or indirectly, through the way the main characters interact with them, much of which could not be appropriately obtained in any other way.

Setting

One more source of information people don't often think about in that way is setting. People tend to think of setting as just setting, the place where everything happens. Those of you who have written gothic romance know better. Setting creates mood. And beyond that, setting can help define character. If a character comes from Rocky Mountain country, the mountains had an effect on her vision of the world so that when you describe that country, you further your cause by describing not just rocks and trees, but the emotional power that lies within those rocks and trees. Once again, just as when you describe a character's physical appearance, you try to see through the surface to what it tells of the inner person, so when you describe a physical setting, you try to capture the spirit of that setting, as a means of understanding the character who sprang from that setting.

If your character is a mountain man, when you write about the mountains, you should in fact be writing about the man.

With that in mind, it makes sense that a setting won't work if it has no positive connotation or mystique in the collective mind of your potential readers. New York, San Francisco, New Orleans, Malibu, Miami all work as settings for mainstream romance because people at least think they know something about the essence of those places. The demands of romance simply can't accommodate a setting like Topeka, Kansas, or 99 percent of the other places people really live.

Pulling It All Together

So, with all that said, we've given our protagonist all the emotion needed to bring the whole proceeding to life. We've got the personality, now what are we going to do with it? Obviously, we're not going to let this fully equipped, emotionally realized person just sit around and fall off to sleep. No, we need to put that personality to the test! If we have written a good, dramatic, mainstream novel, our protagonist will have gone through a sort of trial by fire and will have undergone what I call a transformation of character. We've given the protagonist a personality, and we've placed her in the midst of a story, and ultimately a dramatic conflict, that must affect that personality just as a similar situation would affect a real person in real life. In the end, that character must be changed by the experience we have given her, in a way that is consistent with everything we know about her.

If we have done our work well, the readers hopefully have participated with our characters in the fictional experience we made for them and come away transformed, as well, in some small way.

AFTERWORD

The foregoing pages have shown not only the wisdom, insight, talent and expertise of award-winning romance authors, but pride in the genre they represent.

Because romance novels have been labeled "escapist women's fiction" by many who have never read one, dedicated authors often endure slurs and belittling of their work, not only by some of the media, but by chauvinists and a few of the so-called literati. It has been a long, uphill battle for respectful recognition, and the campaign continues.

Claiming that romance is all about lurid paragraphs, displays of female bosoms and muscular male flesh does grave injustice to the genre. With each passing year, romance novels press against and surpass the boundaries of constraint regarding women's issues. These stories deal with subjects long avoided—rape, childbearing, abortion, divorce and, most of all, love. Love between male and female transcends lust; it is (or should be) the bonding of hearts, souls and lifetime goals. Romance novels encourage and empower women to be all they can be, to reach out and become, to dream!

"Unrealistic" say the detractors. Yet, everything begins with a dream, and dreams give birth to goals. A mother shapes a child's life with dreams of a better future. Each U.S. president began the journey with a dream. And millionaire entrepreneurs affirm in speeches and the written word that a dream launched them on the road to success. Romance covers exhibit "pornographic fantasy" say those who have never looked beyond the book wrapping. Most authors have no control over the packaging and presentation of their work. And more than anyone, the novelist realizes that many romance covers only confirm the criticism. In the greedy chase for money, advertisers appeal to the lowest common denominator in our culture. Their credo is "sex sells." Whatever the product, jeans, perfume or books, they use sex and overuse it. "Never judge a book by its cover" is an old admonition, and in this case, a true one.

Because the subject is love, and most romance novels are written by women, although not exclusively *for* women ("real men" also read them), our books are fair game for detractors.

Since its inception, Romance Writers of America has fought valiantly for recognition of its hard-working, talented authors. RWA requested, then demanded, that publishers replace so-called "bodice-ripper" covers with art applicable to the story.

And though our pleas often fall upon deaf ears, we ask "tongue-in-cheek" interviewers and journalists to not only *listen* to us, but to *read*, or at least scan, our books before setting us up for humorous and often humiliating write-ups and interviews. We ask that rather than pointing out lurid love scenes, they look to the story and perhaps realize that there is a message within those pages.

Mention is rarely made of the fact that this scapegoat step-child called romance has for more than ten years been a mainstay in the often financially stressed world of publishing.

Romance authors spend many lonely hours, days, weeks and months creating plots, characters and settings for readers to enjoy. Under stress with deadlines on books, revisions and "next book" proposals, they find joy and comfort in answering letters from fans across the country and all over the world.

Contemporary romance novels contain subtle lessons for those who must endure, change or gain new perspective on current problems. Accurate research by historical authors exhibits the strength and accomplishments of women through the ages. It is said that to see how far you have come, you must look back at where you have been. Cultural change on the long road to the end of the twentieth century gives testimony to the strength and endurance of women.

Writing is an art and, as with all art, it is hard work. There is no golden light pouring down from the sky to envelop the author with each blessed word. It takes time to create—to put a story in proper perspective, to build an illusion a reader will willingly enter into to live the story that never before existed. This is why we are so grateful to the contributing authors in this book. They have taken precious time to give their knowledge so that others may benefit.

To romance readers: We hope these pages helped you learn about and understand your favorite storytellers.

To aspiring romance writers: We trust you have gained some knowledge about how novels are written—and a little about the business of writing.

To those who have never read a romance novel: Try us! You'll like us.

Rita Gallagher

AUTHOR BIOGRAPHIES

Linda Barlow

Linda Barlow's work has been published in a variety of media, ranging from a short story in the supermarket tabloid *The Star* to scholarly articles from the University of Pennsylvania Press. She began her professional fiction-writing career in 1983 with the sale of her first contemporary romance. In 1986, she received the *Romantic Times* award as Best New Historical Novelist of the year for *Fires of Destiny* (NAL), and in 1989, Romance Writers of America awarded her the RITA for her mainstream saga *Leaves of Fortune* (Doubleday). Her most recent works include two romantic mysteries, *Keepsake* and *Intimate Betrayal* (Warner Books), and a thriller written in collaboration with mystery novelist William G. Tapply, *Thicker Than Water* (Signet).

Barlow is a former lecturer in English at Boston College. She has been a member of Romance Writers of America since 1983. She served as president of Novelists, Inc. in 1992 and is currently on the executive council of the Authors Guild.

Jo Beverley

Born and raised in England, Jo Beverley now lives in Canada. Her first novel, a Regency romance, was published in 1988, and since then she has written fifteen novels and a number of novellas all set in Britain, varying in period between the early Middle Ages, the high Georgian and the Regency. Four-time winner of the RWA RITA award, she won the Regency RITA three years in succession and is a member of the RWA Hall of Fame for Regency romance.

Jennifer Blake

Jennifer Blake sold her first book at the age of twenty-seven. Since then she has written a total of forty books, including *Fierce Eden*, *Silver-Tongued Devil* and her most recent title, *Tigress*. Pen names from her prolific early years include Patricia Maxwell, Elizabeth Trehearne, Maxine Patricia and Patricia Ponder.

Her first title to appear on the *New York Times* best-seller list was *Love's Wild Desire* in 1977. A writer of international best-seller status as well, her books have been published in eighteen languages for worldwide sales approaching twenty million. She was honored with a position as writer-in-residence for Northeast Louisiana University and has received numerous awards for her work. The two accolades she values most are the Golden Treasure Award, presented to her for lifetime achievement by Romance Writers of America in 1987, and induction into *Affaire de Coeur* magazine's Romance Hall of Fame in 1995.

Deborah Camp

Published since 1979, Deborah Camp is the author of more than forty romance novels, both contemporary and historical. Avon Books has more than one million copies of her books in print. She is the recipient of the first Janet Dailey Award, which honors a romance novel that explores a social problem. Her work has won praise from *Romantic Times* and *Affair de Coeur* magazines and has appeared on the Waldenbooks and B. Dalton Booksellers best-seller lists. While she writes as Deborah Camp for Avon, she has been published under a variety of pseudonyms, including Delayne Camp, Elaine Camp and Deborah Benet. A former newspaper reporter and editor, Camp has a bachelor's degree from the University of Tulsa. She's a charter member of RWA and is active in Novelists, Inc., the Oklahoma Writers Federation, Inc. and The Authors Guild. Aside from writing full-time, Camp also teaches fiction writing and plotting the novel at Tulsa Junior College. Several of her students have been published. She lives in Tulsa, Oklahoma.

Richard Curtis

Richard Curtis, president of Richard Curtis Associates, Inc., is a leading New York literary agent and a well-known author advocate. In the early 1970s, he began his own literary agency, and in 1979, he incorporated it. Richard Curtis Associates, Inc. currently represents about 125 authors in all fields and reports more than eight million dollars in annual sales for its authors.

Early in the 1980s, he started writing a column of authors' advice for the *Romance Writers Report* and a writers publication, *Locus*, and out of his articles, several books have been published, including *How to Be Your Own Literary Agent* and *Beyond the Bestseller*.

He has testified as an expert witness in several publishing trials.

He was the first president of the Independent Literary Agents Association and is currently president of the Association of Authors' Representatives. His company acts as agent for the Science Fiction Writers of America. In 1994, he was named recipient of the Romance Writers of American Industry Award for Distinguished Service to Authors. He has written an authors' advice column for *Romance Writer's Report.*

Curtis is married and has two children. He currently resides in Manhattan. His hobbies are sports, music and painting.

Janet Dailey

The author of 89 books, with 300 million copies of romance novels sold in 19 languages and in 98 countries, Janet Dailey is the number one female writer in America and the third best selling author in the world. Eighteen of her most recent titles have appeared on the *New York Times* best-seller list.

Dailey's writing career began in 1975 with *No Quarter Asked,* published by Harlequin, making her the romance giant's first American author. After publishing fifty-seven novels for Harlequin, she was published by Silhouette and Pocket Books before entering the mainstream hardcover market in 1984 with *Silver Wings* and *Santiago,* published by Simon & Schuster's Poseidon Press imprint. The publication of *Notorious* in May 1996 marked the move to her current publisher, HarperCollins.

Dailey has made numerous television appearances, including spots on *Good Morning America, Nightline, 20/20* and *Lifestyles of the Rich and Famous,* and has appeared in *People, Elle, Harper's Bazaar* and various other publications.

Jude Deveraux

Jude Deveraux's books *Mountain Laurel* and *A Knight in Shining Armor* were *New York Times* best-sellers. There are twenty million copies of Deveraux's books in print. Her next novel, *The Duchess,* will certainly account for thousands more.

Christina Dodd

Earth-bound Christina Dodd lives in her car, driving her two daughters to various school functions and waving to her husband as they pass on the road. She is also the author of numerous historicals that make regular appearances on the best-seller lists and only the second author to win both Romance Writers of America's Golden Heart and RITA Awards for the same book, *Candle in the Window*.

Eileen Dreyer

With twenty-four books and numerous short stories published under both her own name and her romance pseudonym, Kathleen Korbel, Eileen Dreyer has garnered credits in romance, suspense and romantic suspense, which have earned her, among other things, a place in the Romance Writers of America Hall of Fame and regular appearances on best-sellers lists. A retired trauma nurse and mother of two, she continues to write romantic suspense for Silhouette Books and suspense for HarperCollins.

Kate Duffy

Kate Duffy has worked in publishing for over twenty years. She has worked at Dell, Pocket Books and Paddington Press (London) as a senior editor. She was the first editor in chief of Silhouette Books, as well as editor in chief of Tudor Publishing and Meteor Publishing. She is currently a senior editor at Kensington Publishing Corporation in New York.

Kathleen Eagle

Kathleen Eagle published her first book, an RWA Golden Heart winner, with Silhouette Books in 1984. Since then she has published more than thirty books, including historical and contemporary, series and single title. Her first single title contemporary novel, *This Time Forever*, won RWA's RITA award. She earned her B.A. in English literature from Mount Holyoke College and her M.S. from Northern State University. Eagle taught at Standing Rock High School for seventeen years, served as president of the North Dakota Council of Teachers of English and now writes full time. She lives in Minnesota with her husband and their three children.

Diana Gabaldon, Ph.D.

Diana Gabaldon is the author of the recent *New York Times* best-seller *Voyager*, the third book in the saga that started with the time-travel classic *Outlander* and continued with the award-winning *Dragonfly in Amber*. The series chronicles the romance of twentieth-century Claire Randall and her eighteenth-century lover, Jamie Fraser. All three books have been astonishing successes for Delacorte, and the next book in the series, *Drums of Autumn*, will certainly continue this tradition.

Diana Gabaldon holds two graduate degrees in science and spent a dozen years as a university professor before turning to fiction writing for the first time. In addition to her novels, she has written scientific articles and some comic-book stories for Walt Disney. She lives in Scottsdale, Arizona, with her husband and three children.

Sherry Garland

Sherry Garland is the author of many award-winning books for children and young adults, including *Song of the Buffalo Boy*, which won the 1993 RWA RITA award in the Young Adult category. Other honors include ALA Notable Book, CBC Notable Book in the Field of Social Studies, ALA Best Book for Young Adults, ABC Booksellers' Choice Award, ALA Best Book for Reluctant Readers, Texas Institute of Letters Award for Best Juvenile Novel, *American Bookseller* "Pick of the Lists" and *Publishers Weekly* "Cuffy" Award for Best Treatment of a Social Issue. Her books have been selected by the Children's Books of the Month Club, Junior Library Guild and Scholastic Book clubs.

Several of Garland's books focus on Vietnam and evolved from her work with Vietnamese families in Texas. She received a B.A. in French and completed graduate courses in English/Linguistics at the University of Texas at Arlington. She lives in Houston, where she is an active member of the Society of Children's Books Writers and Illustrators and teaches a writing course at Rice University.

Roberta Gellis

Roberta Gellis is one of the most successful writers of historical fiction of the last two decades, having published about twenty-five historical novels since 1978. Roberta has been the recipient of many awards, including the *Romantic Times* award for Best Novel in the Medieval Period (several times) and the RWA's Lifetime Achievement Award. Her six-book *Roselynde Chronicles* was recently reissued by Leisure. Roberta has also successfully adventured into other genres:

romantic suspense (*A Delicate Balance*, Leisure), science fiction (*The Space Guardian*, Pocket, writing as Max Daniels) and mythological fantasy (*Dazzling Brightness* and *Shimmering Splendor*, Pinnacle).

Janis Reams Hudson

After working for fifteen years in local television in Oklahoma City and Corpus Christi, Janis Reams Hudson left broadcasting to write full-time. Seven years and seven manuscripts later, she made her first sale, in September 1990. The book, *Foster Love*, went on to win several major book awards, including the National Readers' Choice Award, and was an RWA RITA finalist for Best First Book.

Since then, Hudson has sold twenty-three romance novels, both contemporary and historical, to Zebra, Pinnacle, Bantam and Silhouette. Her books have won seven major awards, been a finalist or nominee for ten others and appeared on national best-seller lists several times. Two of her recent titles are *Remember My Heart*, a reincarnation romance from Pinnacle, and *Apache Flame*, a historical from Zebra. This prolific author joined RWA in 1987, cofounded the Oklahoma RWA chapter in 1989, was elected to the RWA Board of Directors in 1991 and elected to a two-year term as RWA president and CEO in 1995. She makes her home in rural Choctaw, Oklahoma, where she and her husband coordinate dinner arrangements by faxing each other at their separate offices located in opposite ends of the house.

Sandy Jaffe

Sandy Jaffe bought a small book wholesaling business in St. Louis in 1974. The company, Paperback Supply, sold paperback books to retail bookstores in the metropolitan area. After twenty-two years in the business and a change of name to The Booksource, the company now sells books to bookstores throughout the United States and some foreign countries, to schools, from preschool to high school, and to libraries.

In addition to bookselling, Sandy enjoys golf, reading, jogging and, most important, playing with his two grandsons. He's also proud of the fact that two of his sons have joined him in the management of the company.

Debbie Macomber

Over the course of her career, Debbie Macomber has received a number of awards, including the 1985 and 1993 Waldenbooks Romance Award and the 1991, 1992 and 1993 B. Dalton Award. She is also the recipient of the *Romantic Times* 1993 Lifetime Achievement Award, the 1994 Waldenbooks Trend Book Award and the 1995 RWA National Service Award. Macomber served as the Special Guest Speaker at the Romance Writers of America 1995 Annual Conference. Several of her books have placed in the top fifty of the *USA Today* list. She lives in Port Orchard, Washington.

Helen Mittermeyer

All fifty of Helen Mittermeyer's books have made Walden's bestseller list. She has given keynote speeches and workshops at writers conferences, colleges and universities across the country. Her first novel, *From the Torrid Past*, published in 1980, made the national best-seller list. Her short, contemporary novels won ROM-CON awards and many from romance reader publications—*Affaire de Coeur* and *Romantic Times* to name a few. Mittermeyer's book *Tread Softly* launched publisher Berkley/Jove's To Have and To Hold romance line and her book *Surrender* launched Bantam Books' Loveswept line. In January 1996, Warner will publish her long historical *The Veil*, a story about Viking sojourns into Italy and Antioch. She and her husband enjoy life on a lakeside farm in upstate New York.

Helen R. Myers

The author of more than thirty books, Helen R. Myers knew she wanted to be a writer as early as the second grade when she began writing poetry. After winning an Honorable Mention in one of *Writer's Digest* magazine's poetry contests, she turned her focus to novel writing. Her first book for Silhouette, *Partners for Life*, was a Golden Medallion finalist. She has since been nominated for and won a number of awards, including the RITA for *Navarrone*.

A diverse writer, Myers has written for Silhouette's Desire, Shadows, Special Edition and Romance lines and was one of the three authors featured in the trilogy that launched Shadows. A frequent speaker at conferences, workshops, junior colleges and libraries, she and her husband Robert live on a ranch deep in the Pineywoods of East Texas.

Karen Robards

Karen Robards is the award-winning author of twenty novels. She began her career in 1981 writing historical romance novels. Her primary interest was writing contemporary romantic thrillers, but in the early 1980s there was, according to conventional wisdom, no market for them. Finally, in 1984, Warner Books took a chance on *To Love a Man*, which won the Best New Contemporary Author award that year as well as numerous other honors.

Robards now writes mainstream hardcover fiction for Delacorte. Her books have appeared on every major best-seller list, including the *New York Times*, the *Wall Street Journal*, *USA Today*, *Publishers Weekly*, Waldenbooks, B. Dalton and Ingram. Her last eight novels have been main selections of the Doubleday Book Club. Her books include *Wild Orchids*, *Loving Julia*, *Night Magic*, *Dark of the Moon*, *Tiger's Eye*, *One Summer*, *Maggy's Child*, *Walking After Midnight*, *Hunter's Moon* and *Heartbreaker*.

A seventh-generation Kentuckian, Robards lives in a hundred-year-old, supposedly haunted house near Louisville with her husband and three sons.

Glenda Sanders

Glenda Sanders, winner of the Romance Writers of America RITA Award for Best Short Contemporary Romance for her book *A Human Touch*, is the author of over thirty novels for Harlequin, Silhouette and Avon. Research for her books has taken her into areas as diverse as microsurgery, insect secretions, flush toilets and fortune-telling scams. Titles such as *Babycakes*, *Dr. Hunk*, *Playboy McCoy*, *Not This Guy!* and *Scandalous Suzanne* reflect the wry humor, emotional warmth and naughty sexuality in her stories that have made her popular with romance readers throughout the world.

Glenda says she eschews "glitz and the larger-than-life themes of revenge, greed and promiscuity" in favor of "people-next-door characters, the craziness of falling in love, old-fashioned faithfulness and a touch of fantasy." Her most productive hours are from 8 P.M. to 1 A.M., a fact that has prompted her neighbors to tell her she looks like Mother Bates sitting next to the second-story window in her Kissimmee, Florida, home.

Joan Schulhafer

Joan Schulhafer has been publicizing books and authors for almost twenty years. She has worked at a number of publishing houses with titles ranging from mass market originals to hardcovers, from commercial to literary fiction and from self-help and how-to titles to a full range of nonfiction.

In addition to working on the staffs of several leading publishers, she has previously been an independent consultant specializing in publicity, promotion, advertising and special events for authors, publishers and others associated with the publishing industry. She has written for trade publications, including articles for *Publishers Weekly* on romance novel publishing and distribution.

Her career has included work with well-known authors such as Douglas Adams, Jean Auel, Don Coldsmith, Janet Dailey, Jude Deveraux, Dr. Susan Forward, Elizabeth George, Jayne Ann Krentz, Johanna Lindsey, Elizabeth Lowell, Judith McNaught, Judith Michael, Don Pendleton, Harold Robbins, Nora Roberts, John Saul, Norman Spinrad, Dr. Deborah Tannen and Gene Wolfe.

Ms. Schulhafer is a member of the Publishers Publicity Association, the National Association of Female Executives and the Women's National Book Association and is an associate member of Romance Writers of America. She has been listed in *Who's Who of American Women*.

Dan and Lynda Trent

When husband and wife Dan and Lynda Trent met in Houston with a handful of other writers to discuss the formation of a romance writers organization now known as the Romance Writers of America, they had just sold their first romance novel and had only an inkling of what the future held for them as coauthors. That first novel, *Opal Fires*, won the coveted RWA Golden Medallion Award, now known as the RITA, and set a standard for the more than fifty award-winning novels they have had published as of the first printing of this book.

Best known for their forty plus contemporary and historical romance novels and three single-title release women's contemporary novels written under the name Danielle Trent, they also have penned two time-travel romances under the pseudonym Elizabeth Crane and half a dozen horror novels under the guise of Abigail McDaniels.

Some say it is a miracle that they have stayed happily married while coauthoring even one book, much less fifty. Some call it good luck. Dan and Lynda believe it's all a matter of the right chemistry.

Susan Wiggs

Militant romance writer, feminist and butter sculptress, Susan Wiggs is the author of over eighteen historical romances. She has won many awards for her work, including the RITA Award from Romance Writers of America for Favorite Book of the Year. She lives on an island in Puget Sound with her husband Jay, her daughter Elizabeth, the world's most ill-mannered dog and a Christmas tree farm made up of two hundred noble firs.

INDEX

More Great Books for Writers!

The Joy of Writing Sex—Finally, here's the book to help you craft intimate scenes that are original, sensitive and just right for your fiction. Elizabeth Benedict's instruction, supported with examples from the finest contemporary fiction, focuses on creating sensual encounters that hinge on freshness of character, dialogue, mood and plot. You'll also find spirited opinions from some of today's most prestigious writers—among them, John Updike, Dorothy Allison, Russell Banks and Joyce Carol Oates. *#48021/$16.99/160 pages*

1997 Novel & Short Story Writer's Market—Get the information you need to get your short stories and novels published. You'll discover 2,000 listings on fiction publishers, plus original articles on fiction writing techniques; detailed subject categories to help you target appropriate publishers; and interviews with writers, publishers and editors! *#10493/$22.99/672 pages*

The Writer's Guide to Everyday Life in Renaissance England—Fill your work with the day-to-day details that make writing authentic! This lively, authoritative reference is the only one of its kind—a new view of Renaissance England, brimming with the details of daily life—from fashions and table customs to religion and courtship. *#10484/$18.99/272 pages/20 b&w illus.*

Romance Writer's Sourcebook: Where to Sell Your Manuscripts—Get your romance manuscripts published with this new resource guide that combines how-to-write instruction with where-to-sell direction. You'll uncover advice from established authors, as well as detailed listings of publishing houses, agents, organizations, contests and more! *#10456/$19.99/475 pages*

Writing and Selling Your Novel—Write publishable fiction from start to finish with expert advice from professional novelist Jack Bickham! You'll learn how to develop effective work habits, refine your fiction writing technique, and revise and tailor your novels for tightly targeted markets. *#10509/$17.99/208 pages*

Turning Life Into Fiction—Writers' lives, those of their friends and family members, newspaper accounts, conversations overheard—these can be the bases for novels and short stories. Here, Robin Hemley shows how to make true stories even better. You'll learn how to turn journal entries into fiction; find good story material within yourself; identify memories that can be developed; and fictionalize other people's stories. Exercises guide writers in honing their skills. *#48000/ $17.99/208 pages*

The Writer's Digest Sourcebook for Building Believable Characters—Create unforgettable characters as you "attend" a roundtable where six novelists reveal their approaches to characterization. You'll probe your characters' backgrounds, beliefs and desires with a fill-in-the-blanks questionnaire. And a thesaurus of characteristics will help you develop the many other features no character should be without. *#10463/$17.99/288 pages*

Description—Discover how to use detailed description to awaken the reader's senses; advance the story using only relevant description; create original word depictions of people, animals, places, weather and much more! *#10451/$15.99/176 pages*

Voice & Style—Discover how to create character and story voices! You'll learn to write with a spellbinding narrative voice, create original character voices, write dialogue that conveys personality, control tone of voice to create mood and make the story's voices harmonize into a solid style. *#10452/$15.99/176 pages*

The Writer's Digest Character Naming Sourcebook—Forget the guesswork! Twenty thousand first and last names (and their meanings!) from around the world will help you pick the perfect name to reflect your character's role, place in history and ethnicity. *#10390/$18.99/352 pages*

Other fine Writer's Digest Books are available from your local bookstore or direct from the publisher. Write to the address below for a FREE catalog of all Writer's Digest Books. To order books directly from the publisher, include $3.50 postage and handling for one book, $1.00 for each additional book. Ohio residents add 6% sales tax. Allow 30 days for delivery.

Writer's Digest Books
1507 Dana Avenue, Cincinnati, Ohio 45207

VISA/MasterCard orders call TOLL-FREE
1-800-289-0963

Prices subject to change without notice.   Stock may be limited on some books.

Write to this address for information on *Writer's Digest* magazine, *Story* magazine, Writer's Digest Book Club, Writer's Digest School, and Writer's Digest Criticism Service. To receive information on writing competitions, send a SASE to Dept. BOI, Attn: Competition Coordinator, at the above address.

6555